ASSET PROTECTION

WHAT IF?

They knock your doors down today,
seize all your assets and freeze your bank accounts?

James Timothy White

Asset Protection

www.jamestimothywhite.com

Book design & layout: Perseus Design

DEDICATION

This book is dedicated to you:

I dedicate this book to all those honest men and women who, through no fault of their own, fall onto tough times as they follow their dreams.

TABLE OF CONTENTS

FOREWORD

I went bankrupt because of a bad business deal. I owed in excess of $1 million, due to a crooked CFO. Unfortunately, by the time I realized I needed asset protection, it was too late and I lost everything. Fortunately, I have managed a rapid financial recovery because of the relationships I had with close and successful friends who have helped me rebuild my life, strategize, and find my passion. It's my mission and joy in life to make sure that what has happened to me does not happen to anyone else.

I learned about asset protection the hard way. I worked diligently from the age of twelve and built a multi-million dollar business. I was then taken advantage of by a crooked CFO who sought my hard-earned money. At the time, my business interests were sizable and I kept busy managing them. Accountants and lawyers were at my disposal and I figured, *"They will take care of it."* I wasn't worried, so I didn't give this shady character much attention. One day, I refused to take a phone call and had my secretary refer a lawyer to my voice mail, over and over again...

Big mistake!

Soon after, I found that all my bank accounts were frozen and my checks started bouncing left, right, and center. Business came to a halt and I had to fire my employees. With my income cut off, I went broke. My money was gone!

Did I win?

Years later—yes. However, that's another story. In the process, I learned that when property is seized in litigation (especially when the government is the plaintiff), even if you win, it can be years before you recover any part of it. The most important thing I learned was to *be prepared.*

The potential dangers to you and your assets are innumerable! There is the government for one, which doesn't need to bother about freezing or taking your accounts because they are draining everyone's funds through devaluation. You may have the same amount of dollars left next year, but you can bet you won't be able to buy as much with them! How do you fight devaluation? You could try your hand at risky investments,

> ***Here's something attorneys won't tell you because they don't make money from it: maintaining a low profile and keeping your personal interests private from the prying eyes of professional takers—such as the government—is the best decision you can make for financial security in modern times.***

maybe take the gamble and purchase some real estate, invest in a promising energy company (anyone remember Enron?), or you could take the conservative route and compete with the government's inflation using your own investments at higher-than-average interest rates.

Then there are *takers,* people who will sue you for millions because you *allowed* them to get hurt while they were attempting to rob you! Legal rights to property and individuals' hard-earned money have been slowly eroding in recent years. Identity thieves from anywhere in the world can access your information, credit rating information, credit cards, and anything else you might not have protected! Furthermore, judges have grown increasingly socialist and are showing leniency toward the poor and a bias against the upper and middle class. In my opinion, one of the scariest trends is that people live with their lives exposed, and consequentially, their assets are exposed.

With the increasing popularity of social media sites such as Facebook, nearly anyone can be made aware of who you are and what assets you may have. This makes you an instant target for professional takers, like the fellow who took my money.

Here's something attorneys won't tell you because they don't make money from it: maintaining a low profile and keeping your personal interests private from the prying eyes of *professional takers* (such as the government) is the best decision you can make for financial security in modern times. Don't own properties in your own name. Keep your savings in foreign banks where hungry lawyers can't see them. Don't brag. These habits vastly reduce your chances of being targeted, as I once was.

Becoming a target is easier these days especially for investors who decide to manage their capital only in their own country are severely limiting their options. The government wants you to believe that anything offshore is dangerous and risky. Offshore industry lawyers want you to believe that investing offshore is simple and secure, but that it's costly to set up holding companies, accounts, and trusts. From my experience, I can tell you that making the choice to go offshore is much simpler and less expensive than many would lead you to believe.

Are you an American? Asset protection is especially difficult for U.S. citizens. There is a massive industry of American lawyers and accountants selling domestic asset protection and you could easily pay them thousands to form complex trusts and companies. Believe me, it's not worth it!

However strongly protected your assets are, a plaintiff or the government can, and will, challenge that protection. Even if they know they can't win in the end, these people will wear you thin. These professional takers are accustomed to getting their way and they know how to do it! The court system rules time and time again in favor of these people. With the right judge on their side, they can represent you as an exploiter and themselves as the victims. In most of these cases, no matter how you strategize, this simple truth prevails: the law hardly matters anymore.

How does one go about securing his or her assets? As you may imagine, protecting your assets is no easy matter. It is neither as daunting as it may seem. There are people out there who have a vested interest in making things complicated; so if you want to keep what is rightfully yours you must rise to the challenge! After I lost everything, I made it my mission to make sure these takers can't steal any more of my innocent friends' hard-earned money!

Part of my protection plan involved doing a mental past review of what I had done in life related to business. Looking back, for as long as I can remember, I have always loved to do *everything*, especially those things that involved money and business. It all started with a snow shovel, which I purchased with money earned from babysitting. The first company I started was J & W Lawn Care & Snow Removal. By the time I was 18, I changed the company name to J & W Group of Companies and employed well over 300 full-time staff, contractors, and other professionals.

I sold most of my landscaping contracts to other competitors, consolidated the company, and sold the business to my father. The company, based in Calgary, Alberta, Canada, is now involved in heavy-duty mechanical services. This was my first real experience with mergers, acquisitions, and financial management.

A few years later, with the proceeds from the sale of my business, I took a risk, trusted my Chief Financial Officer, and lost my millions. The good news is that I made it back from scratch. However, had I protected my funds and assets, I would have avoided the stress, worries, and other hardships that came with having no money.

Since rebounding, I have accomplished many things, including taking several companies public on various exchanges with the venture capital firm, Eurotex Finanz Inc., which was listed on the Frankfurt Stock Exchange on my 25th birthday. Additionally, I have been featured in various business and personal development documentaries and I have spoken to, trained, and coached many small businessmen and women, as well as having published several books.

I have since founded Eurotex Global Savings & Trust SA (http://www.egsavings.com), which is the retail partner to Eurotex Finanz Inc. (http://www.eurotexfinanz.com) and a conduit for many businesses and individuals who like to hold and keep their assets safe while earning high interest. Having been active in various types of business ventures over the years, I have experienced and utilized many types of asset protection described in this book.

NOTE: This book discusses many United States laws and corporate structures. In most cases, laws are similar in other countries, but you should consult with a professional before committing to making any decisions.

DISCLAIMER: I am not a licensed lawyer. While I have taken necessary precautions to independently verify the legal statements through the book, I am not a legal advisor and my advice should not be construed as professional legal advice. If you wish to pursue any of the various options I outline in the book, please contact a legal professional for a legal opinion.

INTRODUCTION

If you have any sort of income, you need to have asset protection.

Asset protection can be defined as a set of legal rules that help people safeguard their property from judgments. The concept of asset protection has arisen from the estate planning industry and consists of methods to protect assets from potential liabilities. Essentially, asset protection is a means of constructing strong walls between assets and potential creditors and liabilities. Home equity and some retirement plans are common examples of asset protection.

In the United States there are only a few companies and some individuals who are well-protected. Asset protection is the right of any business owner or individual to avoid the harmful financial effects of divorce, taxation, and bankruptcy. The federal bankruptcy laws and ERISA Concepts 36 laws (Employee Retirement Income Security Act) in the United States give protection to some assets from creditors and do include some retirement plans. Though it varies from state to state, all fifty U.S. states exempt some assets from creditors, often including equity in a personal residence, clothing, some personal property, and individual retirement accounts (IRAs).

A limited liability company or limited partnership are also protected by state laws from the liabilities of the entity. Many states also restrict the creditors of a limited partner or a member in a company from taking all the partner's assets. This thereby gives some protection for the assets of that entity. There are numerous avenues available for asset protection. One option is transferring personal assets, as well as accounts, into the name of a reliable family member or friend. However, this strategy is not advisable. An example of a Simple Trust

Strategies: This concept is shown by the example of Mr. X. Mr. X owes child support and also has a lawsuit settlement for several thousand dollars. Mr. X hands over the check to his brother, who then deposits the settlement check into his account. Mr. X can now spend the money from his brother's account and his ex-wife is not able to access that money. In this case, Mr. X is now at the mercy of his brother for control over his asset(s). This is an easy and common solution, but many creditors are now familiar with this and often try to search for assets provided to family members.

There are two sophisticated forms of asset protection:

Domestic asset protection

(DAPT) 45 and offshore asset protection: Nevada, Alaska, Delaware 47. Most domestic asset protection revolves around the use of Limited Liability Companies Principals' Liabilities 108 (LLCs) and Family Limited Partnerships (FLPs). When using LLCs or FLP's, the creditor, who is asking the court to have the debtor's assets turned over to him, in most cases can only obtain a charging order from the court. The court cannot invade the FLP or LLC and give the assets to the creditor. The creditor cannot force the LLC or FLP to sell assets or distribute income with the charging order. Furthermore, the creditor cannot force the debtor to sell his interest and turn over the sale proceeds to him.

Offshore Asset Protection

Offshore asset protection can play an important role in any asset protection plan. Offshore bank accounts assist individuals and companies with achieving financial freedom and asset protection. By setting up an offshore corporation, you create an entirely new entity to hold your assets. It is like creating a new person. Judgments in the U.S. are usually not recognized in offshore courts, and as a result, your assets are well protected. Cases to the contrary include situations where your country has an ex parte treaty with the country where you have your assets. That being said, if the creditor wishes to acquire your assets there, the creditor will have to sue you once again and spin wheels to get anything. This is a costly and time-consuming process that deters many creditors.

Asset protection is the cheapest way to shield your assets in the event that someone tries to take them. There is no one-size-fits-all asset protection strategy, but there are some simple approaches that help you to preserve valuable assets for your loved ones. You must first define your goals and needs, then work with your asset protection expert to devise a plan that protects your property from unscrupulous people.

Asset protection is important for those who:

- have made significant profits in business in recent times.
- are self-employed or are in a medical or other professional job.
- their jobs require them to interact with numerous people on a daily basis.
- are owners of a company.
- have rental income properties and earn income from those properties.
- have anything to lose.

What does the concept of asset protection mean for you?

As a basic concept, asset protection is the protection of your valued assets. However, in legal phrasing, the term is used to relate specifically to *techniques and strategies* that are utilized in protecting personal and business entity's assets; particularly from financial litigations, lawsuits, and judgments. Intrinsically, asset protection is also connected to the financial marketplace and offshore business because many people safeguard their own assets, as well as those of their clients, with the help of various legal procedures available throughout the world. Structures such as trust entities, partnerships, and offshore corporations can be used for holding legal title to a person's assets. This makes it difficult for potential creditors to pursue one's assets.

There is no single strategy of asset protection that can fit all situations, so please seek personalized advice from an experienced professional before taking any action. *If you are not correctly advised on the basis of your current life situation, you could land on a path which is illegal—thus resulting in your assets being unprotected.* Even worse, you may face serious criminal charges or be a victim of a scam.

Appropriate planning of asset protection involves examining the financial position of an individual and determining a series of lawful strategies for safeguarding assets from lawsuits and future creditors. These strategies usually make it tough for creditors to lay claim to assets, view or access a person's assets, or to win judgments against assets.

It is essential to keep in mind that it is illegal to apply asset protection strategies to secure yourself from a claim which has already been placed against you. Once a claim or lawsuit has been brought, you must not hide your assets from the claimant. Well qualified guidance will save you from doing anything illegal.

Basic asset protection steps:

Asset protection is a planning task to deter lawsuits and prevent increased settlements. It is crucial to make a protection strategy *before* any litigation arises. Asset protection helps you shield your assets from lawsuits and creditors, so, if a party wins a judgment against you, you can continue your business with little disruption.

Asset protection is like buying insurance: you cannot wait until you have an accident to purchase it. Asset protection must comply with the Uniform Fraudulent Transfer Act. A fraudulent transfer is a transfer intended to deceive creditors. If the court decides that a transaction is fraudulent, it allows the creditor to seize the assets no matter the structure in which they are currently held in order to satisfy the judgment.

Asset protection is indispensable for everyone who has assets. There are millions of lawsuits filed every year in the U.S. Consequently, I believe that if you are a wealthy person, you have a 100% chance of being sued, harassed, or endangered because of your assets. Following are some basic methods which can protect your wealth.

Transfer the title of your home

Your home is one of the most important assets to be protected against creditors and lawsuits. It is wise to transfer the title of your home. Transferring your home into the name of a living trust will not grant protection; however, irrevocable or grantor trusts can offer substantial asset protection.

Defend retirement assets

Defending your retirement assets is also extremely important. Many people think that retirement assets are automatically protected from creditors; however, only qualified pension plans such as 401(K) are protected by law. If you have substantial amounts in an IRA you should consider transferring them to an ERISA (Employment Retirement Income Security Act) plan in order to enjoy stronger asset protection benefits.

Remove equity from your property

Equity stripping is another basic method to protect your assets. You can remove equity from your property by activating a loan against it. You need to spend that cash or protect it with an effective asset protection vehicle such as a trust. These basic methods help provide a higher level of protection and peace of mind.

Know what asset protection is all about:

Asset protection safeguards an individual's financial and physical property against lawsuits, divorces, and judgments. You can provide protection for yourself and for your heirs through advanced planning. Begin by preparing a complete list of everything you have and each item's value. You may have created this list in determining your net worth or in creating a basic plan for your estate. You can review the property list with the help of an experienced professional, who can assess the exemption status of all the items. An exempt asset is one which cannot be assigned for court action. Creditors cannot place liens on any property that is exempt. Your advisor will help you with procedures of protection, such as family-limited trusts and irrevocable trusts for those items which are not exempt.

Organizing asset ownership in the worldwide economy:

The global economy has been facing major changes such as increased security concerns, the growth of private wealth, and tax issues. Even so, individuals and corporations are still transferring assets to other countries, because transferring assets involves better returns. If an individual or company wants to increase the return on investments, reduce risk, and safeguard assets, it is crucial to choose the right jurisdiction. Asset protection professionals can help individuals and companies steer through the complexities of finding the best offshore options.

There are several types of legal entities in which asset ownership can be structured. Trusts, Corporations, Limited Liability Companies, Limited Partnerships, and Limited Liability Partnerships are the most common types of these legal entities. Many industrialized countries, islands and republics offer special advantages to investors. Each jurisdiction has its own laws and regulations and offers different entity advantages and disadvantages. Foreign companies and individuals looking for investment opportunities in the U.S. can choose from any of the 50 States, Puerto Rico, and other territories. Some of the U.S. jurisdictions are more favorable to investors and some states have asset protection laws. These jurisdictions are discussed in Chapter Nine.

The shifting investment landscape has led to the rapid growth of a new type of business: professional entity management. These businesses assist individuals and companies with finding the right jurisdictions and entities for their investments. They also help handle paperwork, fees, and other important tasks involved in forming and maintaining entity structures. These companies have a large network of relationships and any individual or company seeking the help of these companies should focus on two important points: experience and network. The more experience a company has, the more likely it is that they will be a one-stop solution.

Wealth-Protection Concepts

One definition of wealth is achieving monetary goals. Many people who acquire wealth find that it is difficult to sustain. It's important to find ways to grow your wealth and to keep it out of other people's hands. Threats to wealth may come from tax agencies, estate taxes, long-term-care expenses, and more. Though the threats may appear grim you can build a wall around your wealth by using concepts that have been proven over time.

Even though you may have a large amount of wealth it is not necessary to keep all of it under your name. Donald Trump, an American business magnate, has filed for bankruptcy with his companies more than once; however, that does not mean his personal assets were included in the picture. This is an example of the concept known as wealth protection.

The Rockefellers' concept for protecting wealth is used by many rich people today.

The Rockefeller family made one of the world's largest private fortunes through the Standard Oil Company in the late 19th and early 20th century. No one knows the Rockefellers' full net worth because they tied up most parts of their wealth in complex trusts and foundations which are not required to be reported to the public. The Rockefellers recruited a specialized team of lawyers to manage and protect their wealth. A report in the Washington Post states that the Rockefellers have increased the layers of trusts for two generations, thus making their estates even more complex. They are also attributed with the invention of the "gifting" concept: if you appear to give away more money, then you will become richer and more powerful. The lesson is, instead of having assets in your own name, it is advisable to have your assets owned by a trust or foundation that you control.

There are different types of trusts which help to meet various objectives and needs. For instance, if you wish to remain the trustee as well as the beneficiary of your trust, you can choose a *living trust.* With a living trust, you retain control of those assets and receive all income and benefits. A designated successor trustee will distribute the remaining assets upon your death.

A charitable trust will allow you to pay returns to a charity from a specific asset for a specified period of time. You may choose from the trust types according to your requirements. See Chapter One for more information.

Wealth-Protection Strategies

The wealth you have should be protected from outsiders. Your ex-spouse, creditors, clients, or someone else may claim a stake in your wealth; hence, you need to follow specific strategies to protect it. A lawsuit or emergency may put a major portion of your wealth at risk. The more you own, the more you are at risk.

Companies and trusts

Companies and trusts can be powerful tools to protect your wealth. You can restructure your wealth under these legal entities. You can also use a company you own to buy assets and to make investments. You can control these assets but you will not be held personally liable if something unwanted happens.

Trusts can help you transfer your wealth over generations. Not all trusts offer wealth-protection. The *living trust* is a great tool for asset protection in some circumstances and it offers cost savings in some states; however, some states and federal tax laws consider the assets held within a living trust to be owned by the trust-maker. Consider this factor while using the living trust as a strategy to protect your wealth.

Diversification

Diversification is another powerful strategy to protect your wealth. Do not put all your eggs in one basket because one mistake can destroy all of your careful planning. You can distribute your wealth to various foundations, banks, trusts, and limited liability corporations

Offshore banking

Offshore bank accounts offer substantial wealth protection and confidentiality benefits. Offshore banks may charge zero or minimal taxes and they usually do not report their clients' accounts. Luxembourg bank accounts have been a tax haven for over a hundred years.

Offshore investments

Offshore investing is an excellent option for a person to grow his or her wealth confidentially. These investments are not governed by the rules and regulations of U.S. jurisdictions. Many Americans prefer to make offshore investments in order to diversify their investment portfolios, spread their risks, and protect their wealth from lawsuits. Investment in an offshore company is free from U.S. tax rules because it is not a U.S. company. Offshore investments also increase the difficulty for creditors who are looking for ways to get their money back.

Why Do You Need Asset Protection?

When you have reached forty years of age, you will likely be fulfilling many responsibilities at home and at work. It is likely that you have children's educations to save for, bills to pay, and a mortgage. This is a period of maturing in your career so that you can fulfill your family responsibilities. It is also the right time to think about investments and to choose an option that allows you to provide financial security for your family.

Three steps

In order to arrange powerful asset protection planning you must take three important steps.

The first and most important step is *to be clear about your goals. Then, plan before a creditor or lawsuit emerges.* Finally, plan to *shield your assets.* You know how much effort you have put forth into acquiring your assets. If you want to preserve those assets, initiate planning as soon as possible.

Asset protection should be a part of your asset-building plan from the beginning. It is not enough to earn more money; you must know how to protect it properly. There is no ready-made, one-size-fits-all asset protection plan; every person has individual needs. You must develop an asset protection plan that suits your objectives. You should be aware of the legal aspects while formulating an asset protection plan. You need to abide by the limitations fixed by the law while transferring your assets to some persons or entities. A legalized plan always helps you avoid problems in the future.

1

TRUSTS

Beneficiary Trust

You should not confuse a beneficiary trust with the *beneficiary* of a particular trust. A beneficiary trust is a tool or entity of asset management. This kind of trust is irrevocable in nature, so the grantor does not have the power to cancel or change it once the trust is created. The grantor does not have the ability to make investment decisions related to the trust; instead, this power is transferred to the beneficiary. It should be noted that the grantor after assigning assets to a beneficiary trust, the grantor cannot maintain any control over or utilize the trust property or the trust will not qualify as an irrevocable trust

The main idea of a trust is to build an imaginary legal person who will protect, manage, and hold all your private property so that your heirs may benefit. In a beneficiary trust, assets are transferred by the creator of the trust into the trust for the gain of the beneficiaries. This type of *irrevocable* trust provides a grantor with a way of giving property to another person, while at the same time, protects the assets from lawsuits, income taxes, estate taxes, and loss due to divorce. By this trust, the beneficiaries are allowed to make and profit from investment decisions for the trust and benefit from the fact that there is no requirement to pay income tax on the income of the trust.

In a beneficiary trust, tax is handled in a unique way. Any asset or property within the trust is owned by the trust instead of by an individual.

This trust is not subject to any kind of estate taxes upon the death of the grantor or the beneficiary. This trust also protects the beneficiary from income taxes. In most cases the grantor of the trust is the person who is considered the owner and is subject to the jurisdictional income tax laws.

Assets in a beneficiary trust are not subject to claims in divorce because no individual owns the assets. The same rule applies for creditors. The beneficiary cannot be held responsible for any unpaid debts or lawsuits because the beneficiary does not have any ownership in the assets of the trust.

Although the beneficiary is not considered the asset's owner, he or she is capable of deciding how and when to make decisions about assets and investments in the trust. The beneficiary can even begin a business through the trust and benefit from it, while still maintaining the asset protection afforded by the trust.

Children's Trust

To protect assets for children, one can set up a children's trust. This can ensure that they will have enough funds for education, their first home, or to establish themselves in a business or profession.

Dynasty Trusts

The Dynasty Trust helps with the effective transfer of property to an individual's heirs. A Dynasty Trust is designed for holding assets without any direct ownership; Dynasty trusts are transferred to the beneficiaries, with successive generations receiving distributions from the assets that are held in the trust. In addition to keeping assets for the future that are not diluted by transfer taxes, the advantage of a Dynasty Trust is that you can benefit from the exemptions and protections which are currently in existence. However, you should remember that the rules and exemptions may change if you wish to create the trust on your own. Currently there government has submitted proposals to reinstate the "rule against perpetuities," which allowed trusts to exist only for about 90 years. If passed, the trust would no longer have the exemptions after the 90th year of existence.

Another benefit of a Dynasty Trust is that usually the assets cannot be claimed by creditors and ex-spouses, as the assets of the trust do not belong to the beneficiaries. Also, if you create a Dynasty Trust in one state but you reside in another, in general, the trust is not subjected to the taxes of the state where your trust is established if that state also recognizes the Dynasty Trust structure. You can take advantage of these trusts in 23 states. The states that recognize Dynasty Trusts are:

Alaska, Delaware, District of Columbia, Idaho, Illinois, Kentucky, Maine, Maryland, Michigan, Missouri, Nebraska, Nevada, New Hampshire, New Jersey, North Carolina, Ohio, Pennsylvania, Rhode Island, South Dakota, Tennessee, Utah, Virginia, Wisconsin, and Wyoming.

If you form an asset protection trust your assets will be protected from creditors and lawsuits. A trust is simply a contract between a person who wants to safeguard his or her assets (the grantor), and the individual who is going to manage these assets for all the beneficiaries (the trustee). Beneficiaries can include the Grantor's heirs, friends/associates or another company The contract of the trust requires transferring of the assets from its actual owner (grantor) to a legal entity. For this purpose, an asset protection trust is formed.

Foreign Asset Protection Trusts

Foreign asset protection trusts provide a choice of which country's laws suit your purpose the best, which trustee to select, and a range of provisions to draft into the trust. Asset protection trusts can work well if you choose the jurisdiction carefully.

Getting the assistance of a professional to draft a foreign trust can help you achieve optimal results. Note that the jurisdiction should not recognize U.S. judgments automatically. Creditors who have obtained a judgment against you in U.S. courts must start the litigation again in the foreign jurisdiction.

If the laws in a jurisdiction are favorable to the protection of your assets, creditors will incur more risk. Some jurisdictions, such as Cook Islands, set a time limit to file a lawsuit, and the court backlog in this jurisdiction generally takes three to five years to obtain a judgment. Even if you lost your case, your assets in the foreign asset protection trust cannot be touched by the creditor because the two-year time limit for collecting on a judgment will have lapsed.

There are complexities in establishing a foreign trust; however, they are no more complex than domestic trusts. Understand that it can be beneficial to set up an asset protection trust as irrevocable rather than as revocable. If you choose the revocable trust, the judgment creditor may force you to revoke it and pay funds.

Offshore Trusts

Over the last few decades, many taxpayers in the United States have protected their assets successfully from the claims of creditors by forming offshore trusts in the jurisdiction of some foreign countries—for example: Luxembourg, Bahamas, Cayman Islands, Cook Islands, and Belize—because the judgments of the courts in the United States are not recognized by these jurisdictions. Most often, the creditors have settled for just a small percentage of their claims; however, it is highly expensive to form and administer an offshore trust. Many people find that domestic protection trusts are more suitable because of the expense of an offshore trust.

Family Trust-Asset Protection

A *Family Trust* is set up to hold the assets belonging to a family or to conduct the family's business. This trust is normally established for the purpose of protecting assets or for tax purposes. Such a trust consists of a settler who establishes the trust; trustees who are appointed to administer the trust, and beneficiaries.

A Family Trust is established by any family member for the benefit of other members in the family. The trustees in a trust can be family members, friends, or professional persons. The beneficiaries can be a spouse, children, and grandchildren.

How Does the Family Trust Work?

Once the Family Trust has been established, the settlor opens a Family Trust bank account. The settlor decides what assets are to be put into the trust. The settlor can put a house, rental properties, or investments into the trust. Then a deed of acknowledgement of debt is prepared to specify which assets are being transferred to the trust, and then the assets will be registered in the name of the trust. Family members are each allowed to gift $27,000 per year to the trust. Funds or assets gifted to the trust are protected effectively from creditors and the amount gifted by trust members will be acknowledged by a deed of partial forgiveness of debt.

Nowadays, many family trusts prefer to appoint a protector. The protector is an independent person who has no interest in the trust and whose main duty is to ensure that the wishes of the settlor are followed and to settle any disputes between trustees.

Family Trust Benefits

A Family Trust can provide tax advantages if it qualifies in the family-control test and distribution test. The trust income will go only to the beneficiaries of the trust and provide assistance with protecting the family assets from the liabilities of any of the family members. For instance, if any one of the family members files bankruptcy or is declared insolvent, the Family Trust helps to protect the assets from creditors of that family member. It serves as a tool to pass family assets to future generations.

A family trust also helps to avoid issues such as disputes in the will following a death of the senior family member. It is also highly beneficial in protecting personal assets in the event of a matrimonial dispute.

Family Trust and Trustees

In our modern world where the rate of divorce is quite high and lawsuit cases are increasing, preservation and protection of assets is a cause of concern for all of us. Most families would prefer to see the inheritance of their children and grandchildren develop with a sound strategy of investment and to be shielded from claims of creditors, lawsuits, and divorce.

Besides documents of estate planning and customized trusts, the asset protection strategy of a family can be enhanced by *independent trustees* as well as *trust protector*, preventing the loss of their inheritance to creditors and predators.

When families create trusts they sometimes choose a family member as the successor trustee for managing and distributing the property after other members' deaths or if they become disabled. A member of the family can be a great choice as manage, as he or she understands the circumstances and dynamics of the family. However, the average person has little idea of asset protection strategies, taxes, investments, accounting, and the trustee's fiduciary responsibilities.

A trustee who is a member of the family is usually inexperienced in financial, tax, and legal matters and therefore can make mistakes, leading to personal liabilities. The funds of the trust can even be depleted and mismanaged by the trustee, resulting in family conflict that could destroy a hard-earned family legacy. For these reasons, it's preferable to appoint an *independent trustee.*

Better long-term strategies may involve a trust which can constantly manage your legal, tax, asset protection, and investment purposes after your death. This approach can provide your children and future generations with significant benefits. The trust's assets are less vulnerable to the creditors of future generations.

An independent trustee is responsible for maximizing asset protection for your heirs. In the absence of an independent trustee, the property of a trust can be exposed to creditors, lawsuits, divorce, and bankruptcy. If you wish to secure an inheritance, consider employing an independent trustee.

Grantor Trust and Organizing Your Estate

Many people select a grantor trust when they organize their estates because this trust is used to plan wills or welfare. The grantor is allowed to control the trust property in this revocable trust where the trust terms can be changed or cancelled by the grantor. The grantor trust becomes irrevocable upon the death of the owner. This means that the individual named as legal successor in the trust has complete control of the trust based on the trust terms. Thus, the beneficiary would be legally entitled to the welfare of the owner.

Persons other than the grantor, such as an attorney or consultant may be entitled to administer a trust. If you are thinking of hiring a lawyer or consultant, you must properly understand their responsibilities.

It is vital to select a specialized individual who will work for the interest of the beneficiaries of the trust. They will control assets on behalf of the grantor if an accident or the death of the grantor occurs. If the grantor does not select a qualified trustee to act after his or her death, beneficiaries will have to wait until the probate process is complete. The grantor trust is a separate legal instrument, and the beneficiaries can access trust assets without complications.

Defective Grantor Trust

A defective grantor trust is a type of an irrevocable trust where the grantor retains control over the trust's assets. A defective grantor trust is a wonderful tool to protect an individual's family home as well as a stock portfolio, and is used by estate planners to protect businesses and families. Assets are moved outside of the control of the creator of the taxable estate of the trust. Those assets are no longer owned by the creator of the trust for the purposes of asset protection. Thus, all the future growth and appreciation of the assets takes place outside of the taxable estate of the grantor and beyond the reach of creditors. In essence, this trust is used for freezing the estate of the trust creator.

A defective grantor trust freezes the value of some assets, at least for the purposes of gift tax and federal estate tax. The shares are either sold or given away by the grantor. Business assets are transferred or given away to the trust by the grantor at a price that is discounted, using the strategies of acceptable discount valuation. In exchange, the trust grants a promissory note to the grantor. This means that an appreciating asset is traded to the trust by the grantor for an asset that is non-appreciating. Even when all or most of the shares have been bought by the trust, the grantor still has the power of controlling the business. Upon the grantor's death the appreciated value of the company passes over to the beneficiaries without estate tax. Tax is paid by the estate on the unappreciated value of the promissory note.

Living Trusts: Revocable and Irrevocable

It is advisable to be aware of the different types of trusts. You should know who can establish a trust, how the trusts work, and the pros and cons of particular trusts. For example, an irrevocable trust is opposite to a revocable trust in that the trustee cannot change the terms and conditions of the irrevocable trust after it is has been created.

Every trust becomes irrevocable upon the death of the grantor. Any living person can also choose to establish a trust for estate management. If there is more than one grantor or beneficiary in a revocable trust, the trust will become an irrevocable trust upon the death of the creator of the trust.

The chief benefit of a revocable trust is that it does not require an expensive, complicated, and extensive probate, as does a will. In most cases the court system is not involved in the operations of a trust, so a lawsuit can only arise when a dispute related to this trust takes place. Taxes for this trust are ideal for a grantor. A revocable living trust can be cancelled at any time by the grantor. If properly planned, a living trust can help you protect your assets.

Limited Term Trust

A limited term trust can protect the assets of an individual for a specified period. When the specified time period expires, the assets are returned to the grantor. For instance, a 40-year-old physician wants to protect his savings of $2 million and does not need any income generated from these savings. An asset protection planning professional may suggest that he set up a trust with the $2 million. This could provide income and principal to be used for his childrens' education, with the remaining funds returned when they complete their education.

This arrangement offers numerous benefits. First of all, the amount in the trust is well protected from the claims of future creditors. After ten or fifteen years the physician will receive the funds for his retirement. If he is not practicing medicine at that time then his asset protection needs may be reduced.

Life Insurance Trust

A life insurance trust is a powerful asset protection and estate-planning strategy. This trust provides exemption from estate tax on the proceeds of the policy. For instance, Mr. Smith owns an insurance policy on his life. On his death, the proceeds are subject to estate tax. If the total property is more than the exemption amount of $1.3 million, the estate tax would cause his heirs to lose 50% or more of the proceeds of the policy that are in excess of $1.3 million. In contrast with a regular life insurance policy, a life insurance trust protects his assets and makes the total amount of the trust proceeds available to his beneficiaries.

Revocable Living Trust

The Revocable Living Trust is a legal agreement involving three parties: the trustee, beneficiary, and the trust-maker. The trust maker is also called a trustor, settlor, or grantor. Initially, all three parties are the same person. When the trustee and the trust-maker sign the agreement, the trust-maker is the one who funds the trust. According to the agreement, when the trust is funded and signed, the trustee distributes and manages the Revocable Living Trust's assets to the beneficiary.

According to the agreement, if the trustee or the trust-maker become incapacitated, the successor trustee will manage and distribute the assets as per the instructions of the trust agreement. If the trustee, trust maker, or the beneficiary dies, the trust will become irrevocable.

The trust planning based on Revocable Living Trusts differs from one jurisdiction to another. The main benefit of this type of trust is avoidance of the Probate Court. The three disadvantages of the Probate Court are: cost, publicity, and delays. When creating a Revocable Living Trust for yourself, you should select one of your own successor trustees. You can appoint any family member, trusted friend, professional trustee, or a combination of the three. Ensure that the agreement follows the instructions of U.S. federal tax law. The trust must be carefully drafted and provide protection from this type of taxation.

The revocable trust recognizes three separate conditions of the grantor:

Alive and mentally competent: The first phase occurs when the agreement is signed and takes effect. The trustee has the right to manage the assets according to the trust agreement. The grantor has the authority to influence the control of how the assets are managed and distributed and may cancel the agreement at any time.

Mentally incompetent: The second condition of the trust is when the grantor becomes mentally incapacitated. A successor trustee will be chosen if the mentally incompetent grantor is also the trustee. The successor trustee will take over the management of the assets in the trust.

Grantor deceased: The third condition of the revocable trust takes place when the grantor dies and the taxes, bills, and debts of the grantor are paid by the successor trustee. After the liabilities are paid, the successor trustee will distribute the remaining assets among the beneficiaries.

Living Trusts: Funding a Living Trust

Funding is the process of transferring assets into a trust. This may include transferring stock, insurance policies, bonds, mutual funds, vehicles, real estate, bank accounts, certificates of deposit, and more.

Real estate that is personally owned out-of-state should be included in a living trust because probate on the property can be avoided by your estate. Before you place any assets in your trust, you should consider your personal circumstances and consult with a professional. A living trust offers trust asset flexibility.

Living Trust and Probate

The living trust is a document that defines the distribution of assets of the trust-maker, while providing a way to avoid the probate process. Probate is usually performed by an appointed attorney to sort out the assets and liabilities of someone recently deceased. Even with a will, this process can take time and money. For spendthrift protection (intending to keep one's assets intact) most people create a living trust. The living trust is similar to the will, however the living trust does not have to go for probate, and will not become a public record.

Revocable Versus Irrevocable Trusts

Certain types of properties are exempt from being taken away in a lawsuit. The types of exempted property depend on the laws of your trust's jurisdiction. Other assets are not exempt. It is crucial to meet with a professional before forming a trust and transferring those non-exempt assets to the trust. In a revocable trust, the trust maker personally owns the assets.

Benefits of a revocable trust include:

- Probate avoidance
- Amendability
- Privacy
- Challenges to an estate are eliminated
- Assets are continually managed by the living trust
- Minimization of tax

However, a domestic revocable trust does not offer a high level of asset protection because its terms can be altered at any time to withdraw the assets (only certain jurisdictions like Luxembourg offer revocable trusts with high levels of asset protection because of the bank secrecy laws). As a result, these assets can be seized in a lawsuit. If creditors are aware that you have this type of trust, they can force you to withdraw property from the domestic revocable trust in order to pay off a judgment against you. Recent U.S. court cases have awarded assets to creditors and the IRS in revocable trusts. Assets were no longer in the name of the grantor, but the grantor still had immediate access and control over them within the United States.

Irrevocable trusts can offer better asset protection benefits within the United States. Placing assets in an irrevocable trust means that you are giving up complete control, and because you no longer have claim to the assets, the assets cannot be reached by your creditors. However, family members can be trust beneficiaries and thereby receive financial support.

Trustee: Understanding the Responsibilities

A person creating a trust will appoint a person or corporation to be responsible for managing the assets. This person is known as the trustee. Complete responsibility is transferred by the grantor to this individual on the basis of the trust agreement. The purpose of this transfer of responsibility is to manage and protect the assets of the trust and eventually to distribute assets to the beneficiaries according to the grantor's wishes.

The grantor puts a great amount of trust in a trustee, so if a grantor or beneficiary suspects that a trustee is breaching his or her duties, the beneficiary must immediately consult with an attorney. Only a legal professional is capable of assessing whether or not a trustee's duties have been breached.

There are some specific things that cannot be done by a trustee unless expressly noted in your trust agreement:

- A trustee does not have the power to deposit the trust's funds in a safe deposit box or a personal account.
- Investments in schemes cannot be completed by a trustee without correct documents.
- Assets of a particular trust cannot be mixed by the trustee with other assets.
- Loans cannot be made by a trustee without security or proper documents.
- Cash cannot be distributed by the trustee to a beneficiary without the proper documents.

When deciding whom to appoint as a trustee, it is important to consider the individual or corporation's historical background in finance, how many trusts they have acted on behalf of, and their overall financial stability. An established trust corporation with a history of fiduciary capacities may be preferred to a personal friend. A trust company will know all of the rules, regulations, and ultimately may be easier to sue in the event of error or fraud. Appointing a responsible trustee is crucial to the effectiveness of a trust and overall plan for asset protection. This choice should not be taken lightly.

2

PLANNING

Asset Protection Planning

Asset protection planning involves identifying and applying legal procedures to protect assets from creditor's claims. Planning techniques are specially designed to prevent potential creditors from taking your assets.

Asset protection planning may include establishing a series of trusts, offshore entities, or partnerships to hold legal title to your assets. Creditors will recognize that it is difficult or impossible to seize your assets after a judgment. A proper asset protection plan can cause the creditors to settle for a small percentage or not even pursue you at all. You can employ a series of legal techniques to deter a lawsuit and creditors.

Three Planning Methods: Divestiture, Exemption, and Shielding

The planning can work in three different ways. The first is *divestiture*, where an individual transfers assets to another person by liens or through outright transfer. This method of asset protection relies upon the fact that a creditor cannot claim what a debtor may possess while another party holds title.

The second method is by *exemption* planning, where assets are transferred to statutorily protected assets such as life insurance, an IRA, or residential homestead. This method varies from state to state.

The third method is *shielding* your assets through the use of liability-protecting entities such as companies and corporations.

There are different themes which are applied in shielding property:

Proper planning can provide absolute shielding from creditors and other claimants. The preparation can shield a person's wealth from creditors and other claimants, but some property of the person will be exposed. The planning of property shielding can be made useful through layering other legal protections on the same wealth. The main goal of shielding is to frustrate all the creditors and their lawyers through changing the economic analysis of a lawsuit.

An Example of Asset Protection Planning

A reputable plastic surgeon in the United States was caught in some breast implant lawsuits that were actually the manufacturer's fault. However, the manufacturer filed bankruptcy, so the plaintiff's lawyers targeted the doctor. The doctor, through professionals, had already established a Luxembourg trust. He later filed bankruptcy and his assets were secure.

A good asset protection plan provides asset control while minimizing the risk of loss in the event of an adverse judgment. For instance, if you own several rental properties—as well as residential property—and you are worried about litigation, you can establish a land trust (a simple corporation) for each property. You can also establish limited liability companies to own the land trusts. Another company can also be established to place second mortgages against each property. In the event of a lawsuit for a tenant's injury involving one of your properties, you would be protected.

According to the U.S. Census Bureau in 2009, nearly 258,000 civil lawsuits are filed every year. Most of them target middle and upper class Americans who have a net worth of less than one million dollars. An asset protection plan is not only important for the rich, but it is also important for middle- and upper-middle class citizens.

Asset Protection Techniques

There are numerous techniques that can be utilized to protect your assets. The laws differ from state to state and country to county, so it is advisable to find out whether your properties can be taken from you under your state's laws. Some states have homestead laws that protect your home from creditors. Property title can be transferred to friends or family members for protection, although this has some obvious risks.

Pension plans, insurance policies, and trusts can help protect your assets. Retirement plans are one of the best protections. For example, the U.S. Supreme Court Justices have ERISA plans that give protection against creditors. Though regular individual retirement accounts (IRAs) do not have any federal protection, they are protected by statute in some states.

Limited partnership can also offer protection for assets. Setting up a business as a family limited partnership firm or limited liability company can help protect personal assets from business-related lawsuits. Sole proprietors and basic partnership firm owners do not qualify for this type of asset protection.

Assets can be converted into homestead property or annuities that are creditor exempt. Assets can also utilize equity stripping, which allows you to place liens on assets so that when a creditor looks at your asset they will see it as property encumbered by a loan worth more than the asset itself. This makes it not desirable for the creditor to pursue that asset.

Annuity Asset Protection, Secured and Unsecured Assets

When deciding on an asset protection plan, it is helpful to differentiate between secured and unsecured assets. Examples of secured assets are:

- Bank accounts owned by an individual
- Bonds
- Insurance policies
- Stocks owned individually

Some examples of unsecured assets include:

- Commercial properties
- Motor vehicles
- Real estate
- Business tools and equipment

Unsecured assets need more protection than the secured assets because they have less protection under law.

Annuity asset protection offers two tools to safeguard assets: probate processes and contestability. These two tools help to keep claims from creditors upon the grantor's death at bay. Depending on the law of the state where the grantor resides, the annuity will guard the assets from claims of creditors and lawsuit. Consult an asset protection professional who is familiar with the laws of the state in question.

Converting assets into fixed streams of assured payments can be a hassle-free type protection. This meets the legislative prerequisites and is done within an irreversible pension plan. Furthermore, taxes can be taken into account if it is a well designed asset protection structure. You are also going to receive advantages like spending less time, money and effort. This process can be more affordable than others and retains privacy.

Asset Protection in Divorce

To protect individual assets some couples sign prenuptial agreements. The prenuptial agreement is a contract which is signed before the marriage. The expectations upon divorce and the property rights are defined in this agreement.

Divorce laws vary widely from one state to another and change constantly. Judgments can vary greatly depending upon lawyers, jurisdictions and judges. Every situation is unique and having a qualified attorney is absolutely essential in the event of a divorce. It is essential to see an attorney regarding a prenuptial agreement before marriage, no matter how great or small your assets and no matter how sure you are about the marriage.

Disability

An important consideration which many people do not think about is personal disability. To deal with this uncomfortable issue, you must have the proper techniques of estate planning and legal tools. It is highly recommended to seek the counsel of a professional on this matter before you face this type of crisis.

Estate Planning Basics

Estate planning is the first step in securing the future of your family, as well as fulfilling your dreams, even after your death. Estate planning isn't just for the aged. Planning for the security of your estate means you are securing your family's future. In addition, you will protect your estate from the quarrels that might arise between your heirs and ensure that your wishes are followed.

Another benefit to pre-planning your estate is tax savings. To accomplish this, collect all the information about the different types of wills, as well as the manner of the estate.

Wills

A will is a signed legal document containing your instructions and wishes for how your assets are to be distributed among your heirs. A will can be prepared at any age. Those to whom assets in the will are distributed are called heirs or beneficiaries.

A will includes all of your property, such as land, bank accounts, furniture, investments, homes, vehicles, insurance policies, and more. A will is valid if a court approves it, and the process for a court to validate a will is called Probate. If the will is not properly made and executed the court will not accept it and not issue a Grant of Probate (the proof the will was valid and outlining the instructions). For any person who dies suddenly and does not have a will the rules of the court of that jurisdiction will be applied over the assets and the court will decide the asset distribution.

A will is important because it avoids arguments among beneficiaries and expresses the maker's wishes. A valid will should include the following:

- The will should be in writing: typed, hand-written, or printed.
- The document should have the maker's signature.
- At the time the maker signs the document, there should be at least two witnesses.
- The two witnesses need to sign and date the document at the same time as the maker.

Not following the above procedure might render the will unacceptable to the court.

First, you must make a will, funeral arrangements and arrange your life insurance (see life insurance trust).

Secondly, and most important, is documentation preparation. This is the evidence and plays an important role in supporting your plans and future desires. Begin by making a list of all your assets and liabilities and then determine who will receive your assets.

Thirdly, note how and when your assets will pass on to your beneficiaries. If there is thorough pre-planning of your estate, your wishes will be followed.

The Iron Triangle

An Iron Triangle is an alternate method of protecting any kind of asset, from real estate to even art. It is a complete solution which cannot be penetrated by lawsuits, IRS, or divorce courts. With an increase in the property value and an increase in lawsuits and divorce settlements, the triangle is an ideal solution for many income levels.

This system involves incorporating three entities: a "No Asset Corporation," a Limited Liability Corporation (LLC), and a beneficiary-controlled trust.

A beneficiary-controlled trust is a trust created by a person other than the beneficiary and requires another entity as a distribution trustee. The beneficiary-controlled trust owns the assets. It also owns the company that executes the trust. The trust has the right to purchase property, pay for education and medical expenses, and other expenses as specified in the formation of the trust. If you are the beneficiary, you can control and remove the distribution trustee at any time.

The beneficiary trust owns 99 percent of the Limited Liability Corporation, which is responsible for paying your office expenses, travel, fuel, computers, and much more. The LLC should be the owner of office vehicles, computer printers, copiers, and other office assets. This is the entity from which one actually earns income from his or her assets. The Limited Liability asset is managed by the "No Asset Corporation," which employs the beneficiary. The "No Asset Corporation" can pay the beneficiary's life insurance, retirement benefits, and medical insurance. The "No Asset Corporation" owns nothing except a bank account and a check book. It is employed by the LLC as a manager.

As an employee of the "No Asset Corporation," one is entitled to all business-related reimbursement such as travel, fuel, telephone, business entertainment, and more. Never reimburse personal expenses, as this will make you personally liable for any debts incurred by the company. The "No Asset Corporation" and the LLC work hand-in-hand to protect assets. These companies also give protection from loans collection, court cases, the IRS, divorce, and lawsuits.

Titling

To easily protect your assets and pass them on to your beneficiaries, you may title your assets by contract, either individually or jointly. Depending on your goals, the method by which you apply title to your assets can be the difference between financial wealth and hardship for beneficiaries as explained below.

Individual Title

When a person dies all of their assets owned in their name will be probated unless assets are in a trust or in a jurisdiction that allows no probate for a surviving spouse. In probate, ownership (the legal title) of the deceased's property, assets, and personal effects are legally transferred to the heirs listed in the will. "Probate", the legal name given to this process, is best avoided because the cost is approximately 4 to 7 percent of an estate's value. It is time-consuming and becomes part of the public record. This allows any computer-literate person to access these records on-line.

The term "probate" is also used in the larger sense of "probating the estate." In this sense, it is an accounting process of paying debts, creditors and estate taxes of the deceased. Then the remaining property, assets and cash are distributed to the heirs.

Joint Title

With a joint title, two or more persons are listed as owners of an entity. In the event of death of one of the owners, all items will be transferred into the name of the person(s) who share(s) the title. The advantage of joint title is that joint title assets are not probated, so there will be no dispute over ownership. Titling your assets jointly could unfortunately bring loss of some important tax savings. A disadvantage of joint titling is that debts must be settled before ownership. Having partnership insurance or key-person insurance can alleviate this problem because debts are paid upon the death of one of the joint titleholders.

3

ENTITY and BUSINESS

Asset protection involves applying a set of legal techniques to protect your assets from the claims of current and future creditors. If asset ownership is structured properly and early enough it is possible to defend against future claims. Decide which entity best suits your needs. Some examples are: limited partnership companies, trusts, and Limited Liability Companies.

Start a Business with Powerful Asset Protection

When starting a business understand that owning and operating a business involves certain risks. Generating profit is not enough; you need to know how to protect assets from claims and lawsuits. Protection is required for problems such as claims for damages caused by your employees, debt and mortgage obligations to third parties, and consumer-protection issues. Not knowing how to handle these issues properly may cause the business to fail and put personal assets at risk. A strong asset protection plan can help minimize or avoid most of these risks.

An Example of a Good Asset Protection Strategy

Paul and Karen own a business and have hired a day laborer to trim trees for a client. The day laborer injured his arm and sued Paul and

Karen. Luckily they previously had sought the help of asset protection professionals who recommended that they establish a limited liability company in Luxembourg. The professionals also advised Paul and Karen to establish a bank account in that country. The plaintiff therefore found few assets. They settled the dispute out of court and paid a small amount for minor medical costs.

Specially designed companies offer maximum asset protection from internal and external liabilities. If the liability is internal, creditors can be awarded assets of the company but not the assets of the members (shareholders). The limited liability veil protects the interest of the members. If the liability is external, arising from a lawsuit against any of the members for malpractice or negligence, the creditors may be awarded assets of the company. The creditors will however need to comply with a charging order or a court- ordered interest in the assets; this is essentially a lien, which limits creditor's rights to the distributions made by the company to the member.

To maximize asset protection offered by a company against external liabilities ensure that it has more than one member and that all members are not liable to the same creditor. Design the company carefully. For example, file the company in a jurisdiction that places rigorous limits on the charging order. In English law (the basis of U.S. law), a charging order is a court order in favor of the creditor for which the debtor must pay with interest and court costs. Some states in the U.S. allow the creditor to collect distributions from the company and to obtain a court order for all accounts, orders, and directions.

Another strategy is to include special provisions in the company's operating agreement, including a provision to not assign ownership interests to others (including creditors) without the consent of the members and an agreement that provides that the company need not disclose any information to non-members. The operating agreement can be created to divide voting and control so that the members will be well protected from their creditors.

Asset Protection for Business Owners

Asset protection is indispensable for every business owner. Earning wealth is important and protecting it is equally important. A comprehensive plan reduces or eliminates the risk of losing assets by keeping them away from creditors.

The first step in asset protection is determining what types of assets are at risk. A professional can help you understand how to use the asset exemptions allowed by Federal and State governments. Exempted assets are unaffected by legal judgments and the claims of creditors. Homestead property and tools of the trade are exempted in most US states.

Business owners need to take measures to protect business and personal assets. The organizational form in which the business operates plays an important role in determining asset protection. In a sole proprietorship the owner has unlimited personal liability, so it is advisable to avoid operating a business in this form. Limited partnerships are better than the general partnership form because the partners have limited liability. A Limited Liability Corporation is one of the best forms for asset protection. In many states the LLC protects the business interest of the company from the claims of the owners' personal creditors, and owners' assets are protected from claims against the company.

If you are interested in establishing a legal entity in another country, choose a jurisdiction that offers asset protection, ease of operation, flexibility, and tax advantages. Offshore company incorporation provides confidentiality for properties, bank accounts, and other assets.

In the corporate format, especially for small businesses, there is a risk that the names of shareholders, officers, and directors will be included in a lawsuit against the corporation. Plaintiff(s) will attempt to pierce the corporation's limited liability protection. There may be judgments in which the courts disregard the legal protection of the corporation. Corporate principal shareholders and directors need to use a strong asset protection plan to protect personal assets. Consider using a Limited Liability Company to conduct your business. An LLC has more protection than a corporation and while the managing member might be named the other members cannot be named in a lawsuit.

Asset Protection for Large Businesses

Like small and medium-sized businesses, large businesses also have secured and unsecured assets. Business owners need to understand the difference between these two types of assets before choosing a plan. Unsecured assets, like commercial property, your business tools, your car, and other motor vehicles all need to be protected from creditors and lawsuits. Some corporations are multi-layered and usually have a holding company that is strictly for maintaining the shares of the various divisions within the company so that liabilities and assets are separate.

Powerful Methods to Protect Real Estate and Equipment

Assets like real estate and equipment should not be held by an individual but by another entity, such as a family partnership, trust or corporation. If properties are leases they will not be available to the creditors of the corporation.

Protecting Inventory and Accounts Receivable

In order to protect inventories and accounts receivable, you can create liens. One example is personal loans made to the corporation for working capital or other requirements. As security for these advances, a lien on corporate inventory and receivables can be issued. Creditors will not be able to claim against these assets. The assets are subject to your claim only and cannot be used to satisfy a judgment.

Protecting Trademarks, Patents, and Copyrights

Trademarks, patents, and copyrights are valuable business assets so need to be protected. You can establish a separate company to own these assets and make them available to the corporation monthly or quarterly through a licensing agreement. This protects these assets in case of a judgment against the corporation.

Surplus Cash

It is not advisable to hold surplus cash in the corporation. Keep only the amount required to pay any urgent and foreseeable expenses in the corporate account. Surplus amounts should be paid out as salary or distributed in some other form. Cash can be easily taken by creditors.

Business Entities for Asset Protection

If you want to start a business, the first thing you need to determine is the type of entity that best suits your needs. Sole Proprietorship, Partnership, Limited Liability Company, and Corporation are some of the common business entities, each with positive and negative attributes.

Sole Proprietorship offers flexibility and convenience but is not suitable for shielding personal and business assets. The owner of a sole proprietorship assumes all the risks of the enterprise and the creditors of the firm can pursue collection against business assets and personal wealth.

General Partnership is similar to a sole proprietorship. All partners are liable for the action of other partners. If you wish to start your business as a partnership firm, you can go for a limited liability partnership (LLP). A LLP limits the liability of each partner. A partner in an LLP cannot be held liable for acts of other partners. An LLP is a separate entity so there are some tax benefits as well. Doctors, lawyers, and other professionals prefer this type of entity to avoid liability

A Limited Liability Company is the best type of business entity for asset protection. Properly drafted, it protects members from the debts and liabilities of the company. This entity is formed by filing Articles of Association with the Secretary of State. An operating agreement controls the internal workings and the relationship between the organization and members. Benefits of running your business in this form of entity low cost to incorporate and flexibility in sharing profits and losses as members see fit. As it is a pass-through entity, double taxation can be avoided.

A Corporation is another type of business entity that offers great asset protection. It is owned by shareholders, who elect a board of directors to oversee and manage the business operations. The directors provide high level company direction. Creditors of the shareholders cannot access corporate assets. The shareholders, officers, and directors do not have any personal liability for the debts and obligations of the corporation.

An Offshore Corporation is another excellent option to safeguard personal and business assets. Choose a country that has strict asset protection laws. See Chapter Seven for further information.

Complex and Comprehensive Asset Protection Plan for the Entrepreneur

If you are an entrepreneur, you need to understand the value of a complex and comprehensive asset protection plan. The first step in a complex asset protection plan is to set up a separate company to operate cash-flow businesses. This helps to protect business profits from future creditor claims. Separating the operation of the business from its ownership can prevent creditors from seizing assets.

The next step in a comprehensive asset protection plan is to incorporate a separate company to own each business franchise. Your business can be separated into an operating company and an ownership company to protect assets from creditors. It is important to separate each real estate property that is actively managed. Actively managed real estate properties are more prone to creditor's claims so it is crucial to shield them. Moreover, segregating real estate property can help to isolate the potential source of creditor's claims from other assets.

High-value and high-risk investments should be in a separate company for each investment. For instance, an original painting by Van Gogh is best protected by being in a separate company.

In order to protect your assets, manage your company with a closely held corporation. A closely held corporation is a corporation that has few shareholders, generally family members. The corporation is protected from shareholders' disputes by holding the capital stock in this type of company.

The main aim of establishing a closely held corporation is to offer asset protection for the cash flow generated from business activities. It is important to protect the capital stock from creditors. This can be achieved by transferring personal capital stock into a separate company that does not hold any other assets.

It is crucial to minimize the amount of funds left in your business entities or in your personal name. Any excess funds should be transferred to a separate company, promptly. You can have one or more companies to hold and manage your passive investments. Though homestead exemption gives protection to your home against creditor claims it is generally for a limited amount of the value of your home. Title of your home can be transferred to a company to protect it from creditors' claims. You can incorporate companies for other assets.

International Business Corporation An international business corporation (IBC) is another powerful form that is used to hold offshore banking and conduct international trade and investment activities. An international business corporation can be used to hold and separate dangerous assets located in a foreign country.

There are two main types of assets: safe assets and dangerous assets. Stocks, bonds, and bank accounts are safe assets as they do not create risk through their existence. Rental real estate, commercial property, vehicles, and business assets are dangerous assets. It is imperative that you give more protection to dangerous assets, as they carry a high degree of potential liability.

IBC corporations are legal in most countries. Choose the jurisdiction carefully to establish the international business corporation. The Cayman Islands, the British Virgin Islands, Luxembourg, and the Bahamas are some of the major financial centers for the wealthy; as they are tax-free jurisdictions that allow complete confidentiality of ownership for corporations.

Some tax-free jurisdictions require a registered agent or sponsor in order to establish a company, so individuals can seek the help of local law firms or trust companies that can file the corporate registration to create the company. Shares of the corporation can be issued in bearer form if secrecy is required.

Asset Protection Through Offshore Companies

If you want to protect your assets from creditors using the legal system offshore asset protection is one of the best options. Offshore company incorporation allows you to establish a corporation in a jurisdiction that known for tax advantages and ease of operation. Luxembourg, Nevis, Panama, British Virgin Islands, Hong Kong, and Belize are some jurisdictions that are highly suitable to this purpose. Offshore company ownership guarantees the safety of your assets by placing them under the corporation's domain and removes assets from your direct ownership. This makes them unreachable by creditors. In addition to asset protection, offshore incorporation protects your privacy and offers tax savings.

Asset Protection Through Offshore Banking

Offshore banking refers to the banking in countries other than your home country. Opening an offshore bank account offers tax advantages, asset protection, and confidentiality benefits. Offshore bank accounts are another effective asset protection option. It is advisable to open an offshore bank account in the Caymans or Channel Islands. Choosing secure offshore banks can offer the highest amount of stability and safety.

Offshore banks located on islands like the Cayman Islands and Channel Islands and Luxembourg serve as tax havens for many. Avoid Switzerland, as it signed new treaties with many countries and now discloses everything.

International trust agreement banking is the safest method of maintaining confidentiality in banking. This allows you to open multiple currency accounts. Most of these bank accounts offer anonymous debit cards that can be used to access funds at ATM machines. Offshore bank accounts opened in a jurisdiction that has favorable taxation and legislation can guarantee that income and interest earned on the account are tax-free.

Domestic bank accounts are susceptible to lawsuits while offshore banking provides an unrestricted environment of financial freedom and security. Moving assets to an offshore bank can help savings grow at a faster rate. Offshore banking also allows diversification of personal and corporate banking while providing an international business presence. It protects funds that would otherwise be lost in your home jurisdiction and lets you take advantage of increased banking possibilities. Offshore banking opens up new doors to financial products and services that may not be available in your home jurisdiction.

Look at many types of banking and see which is right for you. A personal bank account is the least protective type of bank account because the account will be in your name and the government can see your name in all international wires sent or received. You can provide a additional layers of security to your bank accounts by using an anonymous corporation, trust, or foundation for banking.

Though there are numerous advertisements online about foreign banks, you need not be confused about choosing a reputable offshore banking jurisdiction. Evaluate your bank based on privacy and customer service. The bank should have measures to protect privacy and calls must be answered by an officer familiar with your needs and in your language.

Be aware that recent regulation in the United States made it a Federal crime if you do not file a Report of Foreign Bank and Financial Accounts (FBAR) if you meet the following conditions:

United States persons are required to file an FBAR if:

1. The United States person had a financial interest in or signature authority over at least one financial account located outside of the United States; and
2. The aggregate value of all foreign financial accounts exceeded $10,000 at any time during the calendar year to be reported.

United States person means United States citizens; United States residents; entities, including but not limited to, corporations, partnerships, or limited liability companies created or organized in the United States or under the laws of the United States; and trusts or estates formed under the laws of the United States.

Potential Lawsuits—Warning for Business Owners in Economic Downturn

Following are the top reasons for a lawsuit in today's economy:

When a company decides to sell their business, the business and the business owner can face a lawsuit if the business does not satisfy the new owner's expectations. In this case, the purchaser should be asked to sign an agreement so that he cannot make a claim against the seller of the business.

Lawsuits against a business from lenders or suppliers can arise if cash flow is reduced by the economic downturn. This cannot only affect the business assets, but also the personal assets of the entrepreneur.

Economic difficulties can affect marriages and prenuptial agreements.

Lawsuits from shareholders may increase if a company does not perform well.

Family business owners need to protect their assets if business income decreases because they are at a higher risk of lawsuit.

Professional Corporation

Professional Corporations (abbreviated as PC or P.C.) are corporate entities with special provisions. This restricts the use of this corporate form to licensed professionals such as attorneys, architects, engineers, public accountants, and doctors. This is preferable to general partnership as it defends them against negligence of a partner. Professional Corporations create sufficient liability protection. For instance if your secretary injures someone while picking up your lunch, you will not be held liable for that injury. A lawsuit can only be filed against the corporation as an employer.

Purchase: Six Tips for Asset Protection When Buying a Business

Buying a business is not for the faint of heart because it requires a great deal diligence. In a business purchase it is possible to lose the entire investment. The purchaser may be liable for debts of the previous owner including unpaid taxes. Here are some business purchase strategies:

1. Due Diligence

Imminent or pending litigation might not be made known by the vendor. This happened to me and is one of the reasons why I went bankrupt. Disclosure is required by the seller in most business purchases. If the seller does not fully disclose the pending litigation, you may be held responsible for the liability. It may be possible to sue the seller, in the event that the seller defaults on this obligation. An ounce of prevention can be worth a pound of cure. Research the business thoroughly before committing to a purchase.

2. Hire the Right Professionals

Due diligence is the purchaser's burden. The purchaser must be in the driver's seat, even with the best accountants, the best consulting firms, and the best attorneys. Professionals who take time to educate you and explain things are the ones to choose.

3. Insurance

Business liability insurance can protect against lawsuits for property damages, personal injury, etc.

4. Your Personal Liability

Avoiding personal guarantees in purchasing or owning a business is difficult. For a business, creditors will generally request a corporate guarantee as well as personal guarantee. Try to avoid this.

4

LAW

Asset Protection Law

Asset protection law is a specialized area of law relating to exemptions of certain types of assets from judgments. Owning exempt property is the simplest way to protect your assets from the claims of creditors. Each state or country has its own laws to define exempt and non-exempt property. Some property may be fully exempt, while others may be exempted up to a certain amount, and others may not be exempt at all. Most of the states in the U.S. give exemption to homestead property, clothing, personal belongings, and tools of a trade. Retirement plans and annuities are also protected by law in many states. Life insurance benefits may also be exempted. Federal and state laws determine the protection available from creditors and judgments.

Only some types of assets are automatically protected by law, so other assets need protection. Asset protection planning should be done before a lawsuit is filed. Once a judgment has been rendered the creditor will attempt to enforce the judgment against your assets. The creditor may do research to find your assets and if the creditor finds undisclosed assets you have no recourse. Plan for asset protection and keep your assets out of the reach of creditors.

Bankruptcy

Bankruptcy laws are intended to protect people from creditors and the bankruptcy option has been used by many successful and bright people.

Insolvency leads to bankruptcy and the need for bankruptcy protection. Bankruptcy provides a way to begin anew. There are three bankruptcy options in the United States. Depending on your country, the laws may be different:

Chapter 13 Bankruptcy: Provides for creation of a plan for partially satisfying your creditors with a payment arrangement over a period of time.

Chapter 11 Bankruptcy: Refers to businesses reorganization.

Chapter 7 Bankruptcy: Allows most or all debts to be discharged.

Filing for bankruptcy automatically and immediately puts a stop to creditors' collection attempts. Filing for Chapter 7 may cancel most of your debts without requiring further repayment. This can also include taxes owed. In certain cases surrender of non-exempt property may be required.

Bankruptcy requires prudent planning. Many have rushed into filing bankruptcy but still lost their property, had non-discharged debt, and remaining tax liabilities.

Planning can produce a structure in which some assets remain for the benefit of your family after filing bankruptcy. Planning can ensure that nothing is owed to the state or the IRS. In the event bankruptcy is necessary, an attorney can provide advice on benefits and safeguards that can be taken. Defrauding the courts will prevent debts from being discharged and will incur court costs and interest along with subjecting you to possible criminal charges.

A few states have specific laws regarding asset protection and bankruptcy, so in these states filing bankruptcy provides a state exemption against all creditors. In Chapter 13 bankruptcy an asset protection plan can allow payment of arrears on a car loan, mortgage, or other loans to prevent asset seizure.

Filing for Bankruptcy and Your Assets

Bankruptcy and the assets you own will be discussed when you meet with your lawyer. To exempt assets from liquidation the lawyer will file the necessary paperwork. Otherwise creditors can demand assets be liquidated. Furthermore, a debtor increases the risks of loss of assets to creditors if a lawyer is not consulted. To move assets from one person to another does not protect those from creditors. If any property exchange has been made within the year creditors can take a look back to see that. The new owner of the property can lose the property if a creditor finds that the debtor has moved the property to another owner. This is called a claw back rule. A denial of discharge can take place in the case of giving away or selling property.

If you are filing for bankruptcy, it is not necessary to surrender all assets because not all of the physical property is on the exemption list. Creditors have no right to property until the court declares that the property is no longer exempt.

Life Insurance Trust and Taxes

Laws change constantly and it is essential to understand current tax laws and to take advantage of current laws before they change. In times of financial insecurity or high tax rates, taxpayers can benefit from a life insurance trust to protect their assets as well as avoid taxes. Generally tax-free growth of the trust assets can be provided by an irrevocable dynasty trust.

Registry of Deeds (Homestead):

A declaration of Estate of Homestead protects some of the equity in your home. This form should be filed at the Registry of Deeds in the region where the property is located. The form requires title or deed to the property. Declaration of Estate of Homestead protects a primary residence up to a certain value. The protection varies from state to state. For instance, in the state of Massachusetts, $500,000 of protection is provided.

An owner of a home can file for homestead protection, but only one owner can acquire an estate of homestead for any given property. Tenants can also file for homestead protection. For instance, if you and your spouse hold a property as tenants, either spouse can receive homestead protection to protect the assets within the home.

Homestead law exempts federal, state, and local taxes as well as claims.

Tax-Free Investments

Asset protection is essential for any individual with assets worth protecting. There are ways to make tax-free investments and to protect your assets. Life insurance is a useful investment tool. An individual or a couple can make an investment in an Irrevocable Life Insurance Trust in a foreign country. This provides the benefits of life insurance, tax-free growth of an asset portfolio, and asset protection. If the insured dies while the policy is in effect, tax-free distributions are made to the beneficiaries.

Private Placement Life Insurance (PPLI) is another form of tax-free investment that offers asset protection. It is a type of life insurance offered privately and requires a premium commitment of at least $1 million. Multiple contributors of an Irrevocable Life Insurance Trust can pool their assets in order to meet the minimum premium amount. The funds are held in separate accounts in PPLI so they are protected creditors of the insurance carrier.

Investments in the PPLI grow tax-free during the lifetime of the insured. When the insured dies the proceeds are paid to the trust without estate tax. PPLI is useful for holding both short-term investments and long-term high-yield investments.

Offshore PPLI is more accessible than domestic PPLI. Companies offering PPLI in the U.S. require a minimum of from $10 million to $50 million as premium commitment. Offshore insurance companies require a minimum premium commitment of $1 million. Therefore, the moderately wealthy can enjoy tax advantages and asset protection benefits. More than one grantor can provide assets to satisfy the premium commitment requirement for an offshore PPLI policy. Assets that are covered by PPLI grow free of income and capital gain taxes. Offshore PPLI's offer investment flexibility. The policy's funds can be invested in high growth assets like start-up companies and hedge funds and the policy assets are held in separate accounts that are owned and managed by the insurance company.

The Patriot Act and Panama

The Patriot Act has been enacted in the United States and it effectively takes away a lot of your financial and privacy rights. Such laws are now being used by lawyers, as well as some government agencies to access banking information.

In the United States banks normally report banking information to government agencies without your knowledge. Personal savings are no longer secured in the same way that they once were. Savings can be garnished from a bank account by all government agencies and creditors who might believe that they have some claims against you.

The Patriot Act has enabled the United States to circumvent the privacy laws of the Bahamas and the United Kingdom and has forced the Jersey Islands and Switzerland to disclose information regarding ownership. Now, there are only a few places which offer actual asset protection, such as Panama, which is a tax haven and provides total privacy for the formation of a company and for asset protection.

Panama has no legal treaties to share bank account information with other countries and does not recognize the court rulings of different countries. In fact, providing banking information to third parties is a major crime in Panama punishable by imprisonment. Panama's corporations offer bearer shares, which allow shareholders to maintain 100 percent confidentiality and privacy. Bearer shares are shares that are ultimately owned by the person who physically holds them and makes transference and secrecy of ownership simple.

5

PROTECTION FOR PROFESSIONALS

Professionals Targeted for Lawsuit

Today's world is more litigious than ever before. Million dollar verdicts were rare in past decades, but they are now becoming common. Taking proper legal steps can protect personal and business assets before a problem arises. It is important to establish a system that helps you to protect your interest rather than the interest of your insurance company or its attorneys. According to the U.S. Census Bureau, over 1,500 civil lawsuits are filed in the U.S. every day. Business owners and professionals are more likely than ever before to be named as defendants in a lawsuit. Some estimates show that the cost of mounting a legal defense ranges from $5,000 to $10,000,000, depending upon the size of the company and the value of the claim. Top-rated trial attorneys believe that asset protection is indispensable as both legitimate and frivolous lawsuits are increasing year after year. Billions of dollars are paid out each year in settlements

In some tort law (civil wrongdoing) agreements, 30-plus percent of the settlement can go to legal fees. This is deemed acceptable in the U.S. but is frowned upon as unethical in European countries.

Protect Your Online Assets

Owners of online businesses should think about programs to protect their online assets. A good marketing program can create publicity, networking, and income, but there are risks.

Affiliate partnerships begin with good intentions but can end in a lawsuit. Service based businesses' main asset is knowledge; therefore company knowledge must be protected. Care should be taken not to inadvertently reveal secrets on company web sites that promote the business.

6

SECURITY

Computers have taken over most aspects of our lives, heightening the value of information. It is important to consider information as a commodity with monetary value. How does information have a monetary value? A credit card company, for instance, needs to preserve a list of customers. Information is indispensable for that company to run its operation efficiently. Nowadays, organizations keep their information assets in digital form. Unlike physical assets, electronic assets can be easily damaged, either intentionally or unintentionally and must be well protected.

Information asset protection is a budding field which involves collecting, storing, disseminating, and eventually intentionally destroying the information assets of an organization.

Security Management

Asset protection and security management are essential elements for a successful business. Risks and threats to assets may stem from internal sources such as personnel and technology, and from external sources like natural disasters. Effective security management can control both internal and external sources.

Asset Protection Scams and Schemes

Consumers must be aware of asset protection scams which can result in fines or a jail term in some cases. Avoid planners who claim that they are capable of reducing or eliminating your tax liability. Every person who earns income must file an income tax return. Not reporting income is fraud. If your asset protection plan includes underreporting or not reporting income to the government there could be serious legal consequences.

Asset protection scams include:

Corporate sole scams: a corporate sole scam is a legal entity consisting of a single incorporated office, occupied by a single man or woman. A corporate sole is touted by some promoters as a method of asset protection and tax elimination. The truth is that if a person who is controlling a corporation is sued they may lose control of the corporation and its assets. Personal protection from a lawsuit is available if the liability takes place against the company. A corporation sole, like any corporation, must declare its income. The money paid by a corporate sole must be reported to the Internal Revenue Service as income.

Pure Trust Scams: This type of trust is also known as a Constitutional Trust or a Common Law Trust. This is the most common asset protection scam. The IRS has warned taxpayers against these fraudulent schemes in which claim bogus tax advantages.

Consultant Scam: This scheme is also referred to as the pyramid scheme. Individuals pay a large sum of money for a weekend class to be certified as asset protection consultants, however the professional designation is not recognized by the IRS.

Brand protection:

The brand can be one of the most valuable company assets and packaging can play a vital role in brand protection. Brand and asset protection strategies help your company protect their reputation and revenue. Brand protection is a task that requires focus, planning and persistence. Protection solutions are offered by reliable companies to safeguard company brands. Color shifting authentication, holographic authentication, light reveal authentication, and confirm authentication are some brand and asset protection solutions offered.

Brand and information asset protection solutions offered by reputable companies provide peace of mind. To stay in business, you need to follow a cohesive brand and asset protection strategy. Though initially it may be expensive, a good strategy can significantly improve corporate brand protection.

Conducting a Threat Risk Assessment

The process of threat risk assessment can be used to determine risk that is related to any corporate or personal asset, but it is generally considered an information technology process. The following security criteria should be met:

Confidentiality: Information must be protected from unauthorized disclosure.

Integrity: The information should be shielded from improper modification.

Availability: The information should be protected from denial of service or destruction.

Acceptable use: The information must be used for business purposes. An authorized individual can still use information in an inappropriate way to harm the company through loss of availability, integrity, and confidentiality. Recommended security controls are:

> ***Administrative:*** This includes management security policies, organizational structure, administrative directives, operational methods, and assigned responsibilities.
>
> ***Physical:*** This is environmental and business security including supervision involving guards, receptionists, and continuous staffing.
>
> ***Logical:*** Logical security control is technical protection that includes computer software, hardware, and firmware. Some examples are encryption procedures, access control methods, authentication and identification mechanisms, and software for intrusion detection.

Analyze the information assets in conjunction with potential risks and vulnerabilities for determining future events. Steps to threat risk assessment are:

- Characterization of information
- Identification of threat
- Identification of vulnerability
- Analysis of safeguards
- Determination of likelihood
- Analysis of impact

- Determination of risk
- Recommendation of safeguard
- Documentation of results

There are different outputs and inputs in each of these steps. Conducting a systematic threat risk assessment is the first step on the road to information protection.

GPS Asset Tracking

The cost involved in replacing stolen assets and frustration can be mitigated to some extent by installing GPS tracking devices on valuable assets.

A GPS tracking device can track your assets. Some tracking devices can provide tracking data in less than 10 seconds, depending on the service plan. Service plans are approximately $1 per day per device. Before deciding on a GPS tracking device consider the following questions:

- Does your company own expensive equipment?
- Has your company suffered any theft of equipment or property in past years?
- Is your equipment left unattended or unguarded for a long period or overnight?
- Is the asset or worth investing $1 per day for a GPS tracking device?
- Can there be insurance premium reductions for installing these devices?

If you answered yes to any above questions, a GPS device may serve you well, since replacement can be more expensive than purchase, and sometimes, replacement is not possible. This is particularly true for one-of-a-kind objects. By installing GPS tracking devices on your assets there may be discounts on insurance premiums.

- Advantages of an asset GPS tracking device include:
- Notification when an asset is moved.
- Stolen equipment can be traced in many cases.
- GPS service provides information useful to law enforcement for recovery.

Hiring an Asset Protection Investigator

Asset protection investigators work for both the corporate and private sector. Investigators are trained to search for lost assets as well as to protect them.

An asset protection investigator should meet the following criteria:

- Be skilled in computers
- Have at least a four-year college degree
- Have the ability to manage conflict
- Have strong work experience in private security and/or law enforcement

Physical Protection

This protection allows you to protect your property by changing the structure of the property. Consider whether the location is safe from crime and natural disasters, such as landslides and earthquakes. Protection can be enhanced through adding physical barriers to threats and by incorporating security systems.

Myths Regarding Asset Protection

Asset protection makes me more susceptible to an IRS audit.

Asset protection, if done properly, will not make you susceptible to an IRS audit. You may be required to fill out additional forms so IRS recognizes the asset protection plan has been done legally.

I am safe with a family limited partnership or a corporation.

Family Limited Partnership (FLP) or corporation offers more protection to your assets than other forms of business; however, if the corporation or FLP does not have sufficient assets to satisfy the creditor claims, attorneys may sue an individual officer or director of the corporation.

7

STATES & COUNTRIES

State Laws: Asset protection planning requires knowledge of laws of the state and federal exemption, bankruptcy, tax, trusts, jurisdictions comparative laws, estates, business, and corporation entities. There are laws in all states to protect certain assets from creditors. These are known as exempt assets because they are exempt from being seized in a bankruptcy or a lawsuit. In some states IRA's are the most commonly exempted asset. Another asset afforded exemption is a homestead Annuity contracts and life insurance policies are also protected in some states.

All fifty of the United States have laws that protect life insurance, but they differ in protected amounts. Some US trends are as follows:

Most states safeguard the total policy from the policyholder's creditors. Some of them also shield against the creditors of the beneficiaries.

States which do not protect the total policy set certain amounts over which a creditor cannot proceed. For example the amount is $20,000 for Arizona.

Some states only protect the policy if the beneficiaries of the policy are the spouse or children of the policyholder.

Few states protect the cash surrender value of the policy in addition to the proceeds. You should consult your own state exemption if you have a life insurance policy with a substantial cash amount.

Many states protect annuities. Annuities are of two types: life annuities and variable annuities. An insurance contract that contributes to investment vehicles on the basis of tax is known as a variable annuity. An insurance contract in which an investor pays a specific amount of up-front money and the company then pays back to the investor on a timely basis—as long as the investor or his or her spouse is alive—is called a life annuity. Many states in the United States shield annuities from the claims of creditors. An annuity is an excellent tool for safeguarding wealth in those states where they are exempted.

Colorado

To protect assets in Colorado, it is beneficial to buy insurance policies. Liability insurance covers the property damage caused by others and personal injuries; the company's assets can be covered. It is advisable to have an attorney review policy coverage to ensure its adequacy.

Inventory everything you have, making a proper list of debts and assets, including investments, retirement assets, and vacation properties. These assets can be included in litigation. Some are unaware of which assets are exempt and which are not; they therefore require professional asset protection advice. Exempt assets include:

- Social security benefits.
- Health benefits.
- Annuity policies and life insurance.
- Retirement benefits, private or public.
- Personal effects, such as jewelry and clothing.

Florida

Among the most debtor-friendly laws in the country are the Florida asset protection laws. Here are a couple of ways you can protect your assets in Florida.

First, transfer assets into a creditor exempt vehicle. The Florida homestead exemption, however, is the best way to protect personal assets. The Florida homestead exemption protects a homestead property where interest added to or interest acquired in it. Creditors holding homestead property liens can attach a lien on property. Mechanic's liens, mortgage liens, and federal liens are three common liens.

Second, remove your name from assets by transferring assets to a limited liability company to protect from creditors liens. Another possibility is to move the assets to an irrevocable trust.

Missouri

Missouri, Alaska, Nevada, and other states permit residents to protect assets from creditors. This is great news for those of these states concerned about prospective claims. The Missouri Uniform Trust Code or MUTC was made effective on January 1, 2005 and it applies to pre-existing trusts. A statutory framework is provided by the MUTC covering most of trust asset protection issues. This law clarified many questions that were unclear in the previous law. The creditors' capability accessing trust assets is dependent on conditions of the trust and whether there is a spendthrift provision present in the trust. A spendthrift provision provides protection to beneficiaries. In Missouri, the spendthrift provision is only valid if it contains voluntary and involuntary transfer of assets to the beneficiary.

If there is no spendthrift provision in a trust a judgment creditor or an assignee may access the assets of the beneficiary. Missouri trust drafting guidelines:

The trust must be irrevocable and cannot be amended by a settler.

Beneficiaries of the principle or income of the trust is not restricted to the settler.

There must be a spendthrift provision applicable to the interest of the settler. The settler might not have the right of receiving a particular portion of the principal or income of the trust.

Nevada

Benefits of Forming a Nevada Corporation

A corporation, as recognized by law, is like an artificial person. It is completely separate from those who own and operate it. Therefore, forming a corporation offers more asset protection benefits than forming a sole proprietorship or general partnership. A sole proprietor is liable and a partner is fully liable for another partner's actions. Forming a C Corporation in Nevada is beneficial because it is a separate entity. The debts and taxes of the corporation are separate from those of the shareholders, officers, and directors. Forming an S Corporation in Nevada offers higher liability protection. Moreover, Nevada offers tax exemption.

Some of the benefits of incorporating your business as an S Corporation in Nevada are: no taxes on corporate shares, no franchise tax, no state personal income tax and the state requires minimal reporting and disclosure. There is no IRS information sharing agreement so there is complete privacy. Additionally bearer shares are allowed in Nevada, so you can buy shares without providing your name.

Nevada has designed various statutes to attract corporations. It offers a virtually tax-free environment, exempting officers, directors, and shareholders from being liable for corporate activities. The corporate law in Nevada offers an overall favorable asset protection environment.

New Hampshire:

In New Hampshire, the grantor does not need to be a resident of the state. Similarly, there is no need for the beneficiaries to be residents but the trustee must be an individual or an institution based in New Hampshire who holds the right of trust management.

New Mexico:

In New Mexico, homestead laws exempt up to $30,000.00 of home equity from creditors. New Mexico homestead law protects only a primary residence. An LLC combines the tax benefits of a partnership and the limited liability of a corporation. A LLC is low cost, has no annual reporting requirement, and requires minimal maintenance that makes it New Mexico's best asset protection strategy.

In New Mexico the Articles of Organization require minimum details: the name of the company, address of the main office, name and address of the registered agent, and duration of the company. Choose limited or perpetual duration as required. New Mexico does not require the names of the owners so names are not in the public record. The head office mailing address can be anywhere in the world. Changes in ownership need not be specified publicly. This is an important advantage in forming a company in New Mexico. It is not compulsory to live in New Mexico to establish your asset protection plan with the use of an LLC; it is enough to have a registered agent in New Mexico. A New Mexico company is a useful structure for holding assets

North Dakota:

In North Dakota, the homestead exemption is the simplest way to protect a primary residence from creditors. North Dakota allows up to an $80,000 exemption to homestead and life insurance arrangements.

Establishing business in the form of an LLC can offer substantial benefits. An LLC reduces the possibility being sued. An individual can make use of a company to provide a degree of asset anonymity. A company makes it more difficult for creditors to collect on a judgment and minimizes the financial and emotional risks of lawsuits. Moreover, LLC is the most flexible way to operate a business.

An effective asset protection plan in North Dakota enables an individual to control assets without connecting them to identifiers like a name or social security number. Individuals can own the assets in the name of a company. It is advisable to make the assets unattractive to the litigation. Transferring assets to a trust or company can protect them from claims. Creditors need a court charging order to gain debtor assets held in the trust.

South Dakota:

South Dakota's laws regulating asset protection are complex so an experienced lawyer's advice is required

South Dakota offers insurance, retirement accounts, business entity, gift, and trust options. It is very simple to establish a trust in this state. There is no finite duration in South Dakota to form a trust, so the state's laws let your beneficiaries continue to enjoy protection from creditors. Therefore the assets transferred to a trust can be safely passed to future generations.

The state does not require filing trust documents publicly. Filing updates and informing the South Dakota court about changes in your trust is not required. State law offers only one remedy to creditors: a charging order against your interest. If the creditor sues you successfully the creditor will not be entitled to receive any distributions from the trust. In addition to these benefits, South Dakota provides relief from state taxes and capital gains taxes.

Texas

Texas is renowned for its strong asset protection and excellent company laws. The homestead exemption is the best-known asset protection law in Texas. When buying a home it's preferable to pay cash. Cash invested in a home can be protected from all creditors using a homestead filing.

IRA, 401K plans, life insurance, and pension plans are exempt in Texas which provides asset protection. This maximizes contribution to retirement and pension accounts to increase asset protection against creditor claims. Divide spousal community property into separate property. A creditor can only take the separate property in the sued party's name to satisfy his claims. Not dividing community property exposes property of both husband and wife to a judgment creditor.

Placing assets in a company is one of the most effective asset protection strategies available in Texas. Asset protection professionals recommend this strategy partly because companies are easy to incorporate in this state. A company offers an excellent liability barrier and privacy. If you want to achieve maximum anonymity have an attorney act an organizer, member, and registered agent and transfer your membership to the attorney confidentially. This technique avoids your name becoming a part of the public record. Using an attorney makes information between you and your attorney private and confidential through attorney client privilege.

Family limited partnerships (FLPs) can also be established for asset protection. An FLP should be filed with the state and you must provide information about ownership. An in-state registered agent must be nominated to receive service of process in case the partnership is sued.

Utah

In 2003 the Utah legislature enacted the Section 25-6-14 to assist Utah settlors to create self-settled trusts.

The law of Utah provides that settlers can transfer their property to a trust to protect assets from creditors. In Utah, the trust must have one trustee who is authorized to transact the trust's business.

Utah has also adopted the fraudulent transfer rules (Uniform Fraudulent Transfer Act). Under this act, the transfer of any property is void if it is made to defeat the creditor's claims.

The asset protection rules in Utah do not require a solvency affidavit but they provide protection from liabilities to attorneys for assisting the protection of assets. A trust in located in a different jurisdiction can be transferred to the state of Utah. To transfer a trust in Utah, the company must be the trustee and the trust cannot be administered in any other country. Utah's asset protection statute disallows spendthrift in many situations.

The laws of Utah give protection to the owners of a limited company, corporation, and limited partnership from the liability of the entities.

Wyoming

A company or corporation in Wyoming offers directors and officers some of the best asset protection in the US. The state has less rigorous reporting procedures, no business license requirements, no state taxes, and minimal disclosure requirements.

Doing business as a company or corporation in the state of Wyoming provides privacy and asset protection. The state has strong laws to protect members and officers of a company making it a good place to establish a company.

Countries' Laws:

Cook Islands

Cook Islands is an independent country in free association with New Zealand. It was in Cook Islands that special laws for asset protection trusts were enacted in 1989. Currently their laws offer better asset protection than any other offshore jurisdiction.

Cook Islands' asset protection law established convenient and flexible rules that allow individuals to enjoy privacy. There are also some specific provisions that assure that the trust will not be overcome by heirship rules. The trustee, beneficiaries, and settlor of an international trust are exempt from any tax in the Cook Islands.

Cook Islands asset protection law deters creditors by not recognizing certain foreign court judgments relating to trusts. The law prevents creditors from searching individuals' assets by limiting the use of interrogatories. Interrogatories are questions designed to help identify property the debtor owns that could be beneficial to a creditor. This includes wages, bank accounts, real estate, vehicle, or other assets.

Assets moved to a Cook Island asset protection trust cannot be seized by creditors. U.S. judges cannot force the trustee to release funds to creditors.

The advantages offered by a Cook Islands asset protection trust attract many Americans

Grenada

Grenada is a Caribbean island state. U.S. dollars are accepted everywhere on the island. It is recognized as one of the best jurisdictions for asset protection and tax benefits. Grenada introduced a comprehensive legislation package in 1996 that includes an international companies act, international insurance act, offshore banking act, and an international trust and company management act—all to attract international investors.

Setting up an International Business Corporation (IBC) in Grenada offers high-level asset protection. You can also enjoy several other benefits by establishing an IBC in Grenada including ease of incorporation. Disclosure of shareholders and directors is not required unless the corporation will be involved in a licensed activity like company management, trusts, banking, or insurance. Bearer shares are allowed providing the ultimate in privacy. An IBC in Grenada is fully tax-exempt. There are no specific legal requirements for the Articles of Association for the IBC; the Memorandum of Association is sufficient.

Living trusts in Grenada can be ideal financial tools for protecting assets. An asset protection trust formed in Grenada provides anonymous bank accounts ownership. Money in these accounts is protected from tax authorities and claimants. Grenada's legislation offers exemptions from income tax, estate tax, capital gains tax, and custom duties.

Switzerland

Until recently, Switzerland was one of, if not the most important banking centers in the world. The Swiss Constitution and banking laws offered strict standards of privacy. Disclosure of account information was prohibited in divorce, lawsuits, and creditor claims cases. Swiss Law did not allow disclosure of bank information to foreign tax authorities including the U.S. Internal Revenue Service. The Swiss legal system does not recognize foreign judgments, including bankruptcies.

Recent changes altered this law. Now Swiss bank accounts must have the holder(s) signed legal document attesting that they have no outstanding financial obligations to the IRS. Despite this, Swiss banks have been criticized for improperly shielding individuals practicing tax evasion.

In January 2003, the United States Treasury Department announced a new information sharing agreement under a pre-existing U.S.-Swiss Income Tax Convention. The agreement was intended to facilitate more effective tax information exchange between the two countries. However, Swiss policy has continued to come under international criticism and in March 2009 Switzerland agreed to renegotiate more effective tax cooperation with the United States and other countries.

Swiss law and Swiss jurisdiction offer immense protection to your assets. In Switzerland assets can be transferred to a holding company. Assets in the holding company can be managed by the managing director of the Swiss company. Assets are held in the name of the company and therefore are protected. Swiss corporations provide investor anonymity but the managing director of the company's name will be disclosed. An existing holding company in Switzerland can be used to transfer money and assets. Contribution will increase the registered share capital of the company and dividends can be paid to shareholders.

8

ASSET PROTECTION PROFESSIONALS & TOOLS

Asset Protection Attorneys

Many people think that only those who have significant wealth need the help of an asset protection attorney. Young entrepreneurs seeking protection for their assets against the risk of their next business venture, retirees requiring asset protection, wealthy business people seeking ways to shield their assets from lawsuits, and professionals with a high degree of liability can use the advice of a lawyer. Asset protection attorneys have knowledge and experience in establishing limited partnerships, Limited Liability Companies, and trusts. They can help organize investments in a way to provide maximum protection.

You can legally protect your assets from lawsuits, collection agencies, and the IRS. The Revised Uniform Limited Partnership Act (RULPA) states that the assets owned by a limited partnership firm are not owned by the individual partners. Creditors of an individual partner cannot claim those partnership assets. Limited partnership logic can be applied to a family business in which the partners are family members Family assets can be placed into a limited partnership to protect them from creditors because of the RULPA.

Asset protection attorneys can recommend appropriate asset protection methods for doctors and other professionals. Health care professionals are at risk for medical malpractice lawsuits, Medicare and Medicaid audits and lawsuits, and medical insurers' lawsuits, all of which are potentially serious threats to their practice and personal assets. Asset protection attorneys determine the best strategy to discourage the lawsuits. Offshore asset protection can provide maximum protection against all types of claims.

To set up an offshore asset protection trust an asset protection attorney can provide advice on the laws of the offshore country. Lawyers can provide advice on new laws to maximize asset protection.

Many people make money, but only a few know how to protect it. Asset protection attorneys are aware of the best strategies for shielding assets so you can sleep peacefully every night. Advanced planning is the key to success in asset protection. Asset protection works like insurance; buy it before you need it.

Establishing an irrevocable trust that consists of a special power of appointment is a safer, more reliable, and more confidential way to protect your assets. The properties that are subject to special power of appointment are exempted from your creditor's claims, judgment collection, divorce, Medicaid eligibility, bankruptcy, and estate tax. There are many types of irrevocable trusts, such as a credit shelter trust, charitable remainder trust, generation trust, and qualified personal residence trust. An attorney can help you understand and choose the best irrevocable trusts. There are many complex tax rules that are part of irrevocable trust formation. It is important to understand them before setting up a trust asset protection attorneys can provide critical advice.

Asset protection attorneys offer assistance in domestic equity stripping and offshore equity stripping. Although homestead exemption laws offer some protection to your residential property it is not advisable to rely entirely on these laws.

Asset Search and Your Financial Future

Performing an asset search will help you know if your business partners, employees, and investors are trustworthy and whether they are capable of growing the business. There are many laws for the protection of an individual's assets however, it is the asset owner's responsibility to collect information to minimize frauds and illegal activity.

Depending on what types of information are required, there are asset search levels to choose from. Basic asset searches include properties, credit history, and the personal belongings of individuals and corporations. Many websites offer asset searches, providing details such as financial ventures of recent years, tax liens, claims, asset ownership, whether there has been bankruptcy, and more.

Online asset searches use modern databases to ensure that details and figures are up to date and accurate. The property and financial assets are verified to ensure the person being investigated is telling the truth. While viewing an asset search report, you should know the negative signs such as:

- Does the person's lifestyle match the person's estimated income? If the person's lifestyle is beyond their income beware.
- Does the person have civil suits filed against them or have they filed civil suits against others?
- Has the individual declared bankruptcy? Although it is not necessarily a negative indicator, find the cause of that bankruptcy.

Asset Protection Teams:

Asset protection teams can provide valuable advice on ways to protect your assets.

Asset protection teams work to preserve assets from a claimant's attorneys and lawsuits and can provide an assurance of financial privacy. They preserve your estate's posterity and reduce personal and business taxes.

Asset protection firms make a complete study of legal structures at the state and federal level to provide the best alternatives. For instance, asset protection teams provide advice on protecting home, automobile, savings, and other valuable assets from several types of lawsuits. They may offer assistance with offshore jurisdictions. They may provide practical tips to protect assets against certain events such as divorce.

Do an extensive research before selecting a team.

Asset Protection Consultant

Entrepreneurs are at risk from thefts and lawsuits; many companies lose huge amounts of money each year through embezzlement and employee theft. Public and some private information is available on the web regarding assets of business owners and individuals. Divorcees, the federal government, collection agencies, thieves, and state governments can find your asset information through online searches. A professional consultant can prevent agencies, thieves, and others who may seek to take advantage of you.

Do It Yourself versus Professional Planning

Some believe that it is easy to develop an asset protection plan on their own. Plenty of information and materials are available on the Internet; however, they may not be aware of the issues and problems that must be resolved before implementing an asset protection plan.

In planning for asset protection it is important to become acquainted with the problems that can occur. Attempting to safeguard all assets may be a mistake, an experienced asset protection attorney may advise that not all assets can or should be protected. There is no asset protection plan that offers absolute protection for all assets. Some assets may remain exposed to creditors and lawsuits. Attempting to protect some assets may result in an expensive judicial determination and may even be considered an attempt to create a fraudulent conveyance.

It is crucial to determine what potential liability exists before devising an asset protection plan. Be aware of assets such as commercial property or furniture in your home that may be seized by the courts.

Though purchasing asset protection materials available on the Internet is easy and inexpensive, there is no attorney-client privilege. Do-it-yourself documents may not provide essential protection.

In some states statutes provide that only a charging order is a remedy for a creditor of a partner in a Family Limited Partnership or a member of a company. In other states a judgment creditor can petition the court and obtain an order for foreclosure. It is worthwhile to consult with an asset protection attorney and confirm whether the laws in your state suit your needs.

Finding a Professional

The important thing for asset protection is the correct choice of asset protection attorney or team. Make sure to ask the team or attorney about the following:

- Are you specialized in this field?
- How many years of experience do you have in asset protection?
- How many years of experience do you have?
- Do you have experience with LLCs and other Corpora-tions?
- Can you help with different types of tax law?
- Are you experienced with Wills?

9

FREQUENTLY ASKED QUESTIONS

Why do I need asset protection?

In recent years, there has been a huge rise in the cases of litigations in the United States. Thousands of suits are filed every year. Proper asset protection planning is required to safeguard your assets from the reach of potential creditors. With the right strategy, your property will be shielded from any lawsuits or court judgments. The asset which is then controlled by a trustee is passed on to your chosen beneficiary. Asset protection is an important component of your estate planning.

How does the process of asset protection work?

Asset protection is the ethical and legal process where financial holdings are reviewed and restructured to get the benefit of legal exemptions by which the assets may be placed out of the reach of creditors in the future. The procedure mainly has four components: the settlor, the trustee, the beneficiary and the asset. An asset protection trust is created by the settler or grantor, where he or she transfers assets to the trust. The trust assets are then managed and controlled by the trustee and the asset is passed on or distributed to the beneficiaries upon the death of the grantor.

Who requires asset protection?

Any individual who has accumulated significant property can be a target for litigation, and effective strategies of asset protection are highly essential for wealthy people.

What are the strategies that are available?

There are different techniques of asset protection, from the simple to the complex. No particular strategy is able to cover each and every option. Different asset protection techniques of are applicable in various situations. However, in general, a plan for asset protection involves certain legal exemptions and several entities for protection.

Why should I utilize an offshore trust?

An offshore trust is used for higher secrecy. In such a case, your asset(s) is/are transferred to a trust in a foreign country. Asset protection legislation has been enacted by many countries like the Bahamas, Cayman Islands, Mauritius, Cook Island, Belize and more. In an offshore trust, your assets are more secure since they cannot easily be reached by the courts in the United States. This makes it very difficult for the creditors to get in touch with your property.

10

CONCLUSION

Asset protection planning is serious business, requiring careful thought. Most often, trusts form an important part of an asset protection program. It is essential to start now, before it is too late, and to be prepared by paying for good, quality guidance and advice. Your asset protection plan should include giving up control over a portion of your assets and ensuring that your record is completely clean and up to date.

Trusts play a vital role in planning, though in many cases, life insurances, LLC's and other corporate structures can work as viable alternatives. Moreover, you can benefit from a combination of these structures, which may be more effective than a pure structure of a trust. Proper tax and legal advice ensure that your property is protected appropriately.

We will be pleased to guide you to our associates, who can help you to achieve your asset protection needs. Visit us at: www.egsavings.com or contact us at info@egsavings.com, or call us from North America at (888)-420-0164 or from Europe at +352-800-2-7972.

TERMS, DEFINITIONS AND GLOSSARY:

A/B Trust - A type of Revocable Living Trust used by married couples. In this type of living trust, two trusts (trust A and trust B) are created at the time the first spouse dies. By dividing the couple's estate into two trusts at the first death, each spouse can pass the maximum amount of property allowed to avoid federal estate taxes. One trust, usually trust A, is often referred to as the marital deduction trust and the other trust, usually trust B, is often referred to as the shelter trust.

Accumulation Trust - A type of trust which retains and accumulates income for longer than a year, instead of paying all of the income out to the beneficiaries at least annually. These types of trusts are also known as complex trusts.

Administrator - The person designated by the court to manage and distribute a probate estate when there isn't a will. If there is a will, the person so designated is called the executor (male), executrix (female), or personal representative.

Adult - Any person over the age of 18 or 21. The age of an adult depends on specific state laws.

Affidavit - A sworn, written statement executed under oath in front of a witness or witnesses.

Affidavit of Domicile - A sworn, written statement verifying city, county and state of residence.

Affidavit of Survivorship - A sworn, written statement verifying the identity of the survivor in a joint tenancy or other property ownership relationship.

Ancillary Probate - A probate proceeding conducted in a state other than the state where the decedent lived and the primary probate occurs.

Annual Exclusion - The amount of property the IRS allows a person to gift to another person during a calendar year before a gift tax is assessed and/or a gift tax return must be filed. The amount is increased periodically. There is no limit to the number of people you can give gifts to who qualify for the annual exclusion. To qualify for the annual exclusion, the gift must be one that a recipient can enjoy immediately and have full control over.

Ante-nuptial Agreement - A contract between two potential marriage partners specifying how the property owned by each prior to marriage and owned individually or jointly during marriage will be divided should the couple divorce.

Ascertainable Standard - The IRS-defined standard which governs the use of trust B property and prevents the property from being considered part of the trustee's property for estate tax purposes. The standard is defined as "health, education, maintenance and support" of the surviving spouse and children.

Asset Protection - Protecting your property from legal problems and taxes during your life and after your death.

Basis - A tax term which refers to the original or acquisition value of a property, used to determine the amount of tax that will be assessed. The basis is deducted from the sales price of the property, when it is sold, to determine the profit or loss.

Beneficiary - The person(s) or organization(s) who receive(s) the benefits of trust property held under the terms of a trust.

Bequest - An old legal term meaning to give a gift or leave property under the terms of a will.

Bond - An insurance policy used to ensure a legal representative will do his job and not misuse or steal funds he is controlling. The bond guarantees that a certain amount of money will be paid if a party is injured due to acts of the legal representative.

By Right of Representation - Common terminology for the Latin term, Per Stirpes. This is the most common way of distributing an estate such that if one of the children is dead, his children share equally in his share of the estate distribution. This term is often summarized by the phrase, "if the parent is dead, his children stand in his shoes."

Charitable Remainder Trust - A trust used to make large donations of property or money to a charity, so the person making the gift or donation can obtain a tax advantage. In a charitable remainder trust, the donor reserves the right to use the trust property during his life or some other specified time period and, when the agreed period is over, the property goes to the charity.

Codicil - A written change or amendment to a will.

Community Property - Some state laws require that all assets acquired during a marriage belong equally to both spouses, except for gifts and inheritances given specifically to one spouse. The eight states with such laws are known as community property states. The eight states are Arizona, California, Idaho, Louisiana, Nevada, New Mexico, Texas and Washington. Puerto Rico also uses the community property system, and Wisconsin has a modified community property system.

Complex Trust - See Accumulation Trust

Conservator - A person appointed to be legally responsible for the management of property and money belonging to a minor or incompetent person. The conservator may act as the guardian or the guardian may be a separate person and the conservator will just work with the guardian.

Conservatorship - A court-controlled program where a conservator is appointed by the court to manage the monetary affairs of a person(s) who is/are unable to manage his/her own affairs.

Contract - An agreement between two or more parties. It may be oral, but, generally, it is written.

Creditor - A person or institution to which money is owed.

Custodial Parent - The parent given custody and responsibility by the divorce court for the children of the divorced couple.

Decedent - The person who has died.

Death taxes - Taxes levied on the property of a deceased person. Federal death taxes are usually referred to as estate taxes. Local and state death taxes are often referred to as inheritance taxes or simply death taxes.

Deed - A written document used to show ownership and/or transfer title to real estate.

Debtor - A person who owes money.

Devise - A legal term referring to real estate which passes through a will.

Disclaimer - The refusal of a beneficiary to accept property willed to him. When a disclaimer is made, the property is generally transferred to the person next in line under the will. A disclaimer is also called a renunciation.

Dispositive Provision - A clause in a will or trust that gives away property.

Disposition - The parting with or giving away of property.

Disinherit - Cutting a person off from his or her inheritance in an estate where he or she would have been a natural heir.

Doctrine of Independent Significance - The legal power to make reference in one document to an independent document that stands alone. By making reference to the independent document, the law will allow the independent document to be incorporated into the document making reference to it.

Domicile - The state or county which is the primary residence of a person.

Donee - A person who receives a gift.

Donor - A person who makes a gift.

Durable Power of Attorney - A document established by an individual (the principal) granting another person (the agent) the right and authority to handle the financial and other affairs of the principal. The Durable Power of Attorney survives through the period of incompetency of the principal.

Durable Power of Attorney for Health Care - A document established by an individual (the principal) granting another person (the agent) the right and authority to handle matters related to the health care of the principal.

Due-on-sale Clause - A clause in a mortgage document which requires that the mortgage be paid in full if the encumbered property is transferred.

Escheat - A legal word that describes the situation where property transfers to the ownership of the state government because there are no legal inheritors to claim it.

Estate - The aggregate of all assets and debts held (owned) by an individual during his or her life or at the time of his or her death.

Estate Taxes - Taxes imposed on the "privilege" of transferring property by reason of death. Estate tax is most commonly used in reference to the tax imposed by the Federal Government rather than the state government. Estate taxes are intended to raise revenue for the government and break up a family's wealth, so that the nation's wealth doesn't concentrate in the hands of a few families.

Executor/ Executrix - The person (male/female) named in a will to manage a decedent's estate. The more modern term is a "personal representative," which removes any reference to the sex of the person.

Exemption Equivalent - When property is given as a gift or passed to heirs as part of an estate, it is subject to federal estate and gift tax laws. Each person is given a tax credit (the "unified credit") that can be used to offset the tax assessed against a specific amount of property. The amount of property that results in a tax exactly equal to the unified credit is known as the "exemption equivalent." Technically, no property is exempt from federal estate and gift taxes, but the term exemption equivalent is commonly used. Stated another way, the unified credit is equal to the amount of tax due on a gift or estate transfer of property that has a value equal to the exemption equivalent amount.

Family Trust - Another name for a living trust.

Fiduciary - A person with the legal duty to act primarily for another's benefit in a position of trust, good faith, candor and responsibility. "Fiduciary" is often used as an alternative term for "trustee."

Fiduciary Duty - The duty of a fiduciary to act in a position of trust, good faith, candor and responsibility, on behalf of another. The duty is one of the best-defined responsibilities under the law and is very strictly enforced by the courts.

Fraud - The use of deception for unlawful gain.

General Power of Attorney - A legal document that, when properly executed, gives one person (the agent) full, legal authority to act on behalf of another (the principal). The scope of the document can be as broad or narrow as you desire, as defined in the document. A general power of attorney becomes invalid when the principal dies or becomes incompetent.

Gift - A transfer of property without receiving some benefit in return. The person making the transfer cannot be obligated in any way to make the transfer.

Gift Taxes - Taxes levied by the Federal Government on gifts. Gift taxes and estate taxes have been "merged" into a single tax called the "unified tax."

Grantor - The person who establishes a trust and transfers assets into it. Other terms for the "grantor" include "trustor" and "settlor."

Grantor Trust - A trust in which the person establishing the trust retains enough "ownership rights" or "incidents of ownership" that the person is treated by the IRS as the owner of the trust assets for tax purposes. The right to revoke the trust is sufficient to make the trust a grantor trust.

Gross Estate - The total value of an estate at the date of the decedent's death. The value is determined before debts and other "deductions" are subtracted from the estate value.

Guarantor - A party who guarantees repayment of a loan, using his/her own assets if necessary.

Guardian - A person designated by court appointment and given the responsibility of managing the personal affairs of a minor child or a person who is legally incompetent to manage his or her own affairs.

Heir - A person who, by law, inherits property from a deceased relative who didn't leave any type of will or trust which distributes his or her property after death. The term is more "loosely" used to refer to a person who receives property from a decedent through any means.

Heirloom - A personal possession that usually has a sentimental value which exceeds its monetary value.

Holographic Will - A do-it-yourself, handwritten will. To be valid, this will must be totally in your own handwriting, signed and dated. About 20 states allow holographic wills, but it is best to have a more formal will.

Homestead Laws - State laws which protect your house, clothing, and personal property, up to a specific dollar amount, from being taken away by most types of lawsuits or bankruptcies.

Household Items - The phrase in a will which indicates everything that may be used for the convenience of the house, such as tables, chairs, bedding, etc. Apparel, books, weapons, and the like are not included.

Incapacitated - A person who is legally incapable of managing his or her own business affairs. A person may be permanently or temporarily incapacitated. A probate court usually decides if a person is incapacitated or not. "Incapacitated" is often used interchangeably with "incompetent."

Incidents of Ownership - All or any management control over a trust or an insurance policy. In relation to an insurance policy, incidents of ownership include the right to change the beneficiaries, borrow cash value, and change the ownership, among other rights.

Income Tax - A tax assessed on gain made by an individual or entity.

Incompetent - A person who is legally incapable of managing his or her own business affairs. A person may be permanently or temporarily incompetent. A probate court usually decides if a person is incompetent or not. "Incompetent" is often used interchangeably with "incapacitated."

Independent Trustee - A trustee who is unrelated to the person who establishes a trust (the grantor) and the beneficiaries of the trust. Unrelated attorneys, banks, corporations, etc., are usually chosen to act as independent trustees. The IRS requires a trust to have an independent trustee if the trust is to achieve certain estate tax and income tax benefits available to irrevocable trusts (not living trusts).

Inherit - To take or receive property by legal right from a deceased person.

Inheritance Tax - A tax imposed upon the transfer of property from a deceased person's estate. "Inheritance Tax" is a term which is usually applied to the taxes charged by a state, while the taxes imposed by the Federal Government are usually referred to as estate taxes.

Inter Vivos Revocable Trust - One name for a living trust. "Inter vivos" is Latin for "between the living."

Intestate - To die without a will or other valid estate-transfer devise.

Intestate Succession - The order of persons entitled to received property distributed by a state court when the deceased failed to write a will or trust, or the will or trust has failed to legally distribute the deceased person's property.

Irrevocable Trust - A trust that cannot be changed, canceled, or revoked once it is set up. A "living trust" is not an example of an irrevocable trust. Insurance trusts and "Children's Trusts," or "2503 Trusts," are examples of irrevocable trusts. Irrevocable trusts are treated by the IRS very differently than revocable trusts.

Insurance Trust - An irrevocable trust used to hold insurance and pass it on to one's heirs without any estate taxes on the death benefits of the policy.

Issue - A legal term used in wills and trusts meaning one's children, grandchildren, etc., either through birth or adoption.

Joint Ownership - The situation where two or more people own the same piece of property together. The property can be "owned" by the people as joint tenants, tenants in common, tenants by the entirety and other legally-defined relationships.

Joint Tenancy - When two or more people take title to the same property and simultaneously each owns 100% of the property or has full rights to the property. At the death of one joint tenant, his or her share immediately transfers to the ownership of the survivor(s).

Jurisdiction - The location where a person has access to the court system. The place where a person lives usually determines which court has the legal right to adjudicate his or her claims, probate proceedings, or other matters. The location of real property can also determine the "jurisdiction" of legal matters related to that property.

Letters Testamentary - A formal court order (document) issued by a probate judge giving the personal representative authority to conduct business, contract, sell estate property, pay bills, distribute estate property, and otherwise act on behalf of the estate.

Life Estate - The right to have all of the benefit from a property during one's lifetime. The person with the right doesn't own the property, and when he or she dies, the property is not included in his or her estate.

Life Insurance Trust - A type of irrevocable trust used to hold life insurance. When a life insurance policy is held in an insurance trust, it is protected from estate taxes when the insured dies, provided the trust is established properly, managed properly, and the insured does not retain any "incidents of ownership."

Living Trust - A type of revocable trust used in estate planning to avoid probate, help in situations of incompetency, and allow "smooth" management of assets after the death of the grantor or person who established the trust. The trust can be effective in eliminating or reducing estate taxes for married couples. Revocable living trusts are established during the life of the grantor, who retains the right to the income and principal and the right to amend or revoke the trust. When the grantor dies, the trust becomes irrevocable and acts as a substitute for a traditional will.

Living Will - A document defining your "right to die." It usually states that you do not want to have your life artificially prolonged by modern, medical technologies. You can specifically define the means which you do not want used or do want used.

Lunch Theory of Justice - Lee's theory concerning the way courts dispense justice, i.e., the outcome of a case depends on what the judge or jury ate for lunch.

Loving Trust - Another name for a living trust. The term "loving trust" was popularized in the 1980's by a group selling living trusts.

Marital Deduction - The unlimited deduction allowed under federal estate tax law for all qualifying property passing from the estate of the deceased spouse to the surviving spouse. The value of the property passing to the surviving spouse under the marital deduction is "deducted" from the deceased spouse's estate before federal estate taxes are calculated on the estate. Proper planning and use of the deduction allows more property to pass estate tax-free to the family.

Marital Deduction Trust - The trust which "receives" the property passed under the marital deduction laws from the deceased spouse's estate to the surviving spouse. Property in the marital deduction trust will be included as part of the surviving spouse's estate (for estate tax purposes) when he or she dies.

Minor - A child who is not old enough to have the legal capacity to govern his or her own affairs. Depending upon the specific state and the specific laws being applied, a minor is usually either under 21 years old or 18 years old.

Net Taxable Estate - The value of an estate upon which the federal estate tax is levied. The net taxable estate or "net value" is the total or "gross value" of the estate less liabilities, expenses and other deductions allowed by the tax laws.

Notice - The legally prescribed process of making someone aware of a legal proceeding or matter.

Notarized - The affirmation of an agent (the notary) of the state affirming that the signature on the document being "notarized" is, in fact, the signature of the person purportedly signing the document.

Notary - A person who has state-granted authority to certify the validity or authenticity of the signature being made on a document.

Pay on Death Account - See POD Account.

Per Capita - A method of distributing an estate such that all of the surviving descendants share equally in the property. Also known as Pro Rata.

Per Stirpes - The most common way of distributing an estate such that if one of the children is dead, his or her children share equally in his or her share. Also known as "By Right of Representation."

Perpetuities Savings Clause - A "safety net" clause included in most trusts, which automatically terminates the trust at the last possible moment to prevent any possible violation of trust law caused because the general terms of the trust did not properly provide for a termination of the trust as required by law. Under most state laws, a trust must have a finite "life" and end prior to the time required by law.

Personal Letter - A letter directing the distribution of personal items. This letter is referenced in a person's will and is recognized by the courts upon the death of the person making the will and letter.

Personal Property - Property other than real estate (land and permanent structures on the land). Cars, furniture, securities, bank accounts, and animals are examples of personal property.

Personal Representative - The "modern" term for the executor or executrix, who is the court-appointed individual who probates the will and carries out the will's instructions under court supervision.

POD Account - A bank account that is designed to avoid probate. It is a contract between the bank and the account holder guaranteeing that, upon the account holder's death, the bank will pay the balance of the account to whomever is designated to receive the account.

Pour-over Trust - A trust designed to receive property that is "poured-over" into it. The property is usually "poured over" or received from a pour-over will through the probate process. See Pour-over Will.

Pour-over Will - A will which contains a clause that transfers some or all of the assets that pass through the will into a trust for final distribution from the trust. The will's assets are said to "pour-over" into the trust.

Power of Appointment - The power given to a person, by appointment in a will or a trust, to distribute the property that passes through the will or trust at the discretion of the person appointed. Other than to give the appointed person the authority to make the distribution, the will or trust doesn't make distribution of the property.

Power of Attorney - A document established by an individual (the principal) granting another person (the agent) the right and authority to handle the financial affairs for the principal. A power of attorney becomes invalid at the death or incompetency of the principal, unless the power of attorney is a "durable power of attorney" which remains in effect after the principal becomes incompetent.

Prenuptial Agreement - A contract between two potential marriage partners specifying how the property owned by each prior to marriage and owned individually or jointly during marriage will be divided should the couple divorce.

Primary Beneficiary - The person or persons for whose benefit a trust is originally established. When conditions change and the primary beneficiaries are no longer in a position to receive the benefit of the trust, the benefit goes to the "secondary beneficiaries."

Probate - The legal process which facilitates the transfer of a deceased person's property, whether they leave a will or don't leave any will. The court establishes the authenticity of the will (if any), appoints a personal representative or administrator, identifies heirs and creditors, directs payment of debts and taxes, and oversees distributions of the assets according to the will or state law in the absence of a will.

Probate Court - The part of the judicial system dedicated to handling probate matters, which includes settlement of intestate and testate estates, adoptions, appointment of guardians, name changes, and other matters.

Probate Estate - A deceased person's property which is subject to the probate process. Property held in a living trust is usually not considered part of the probate estate.

Probate Fees - The fees, often a percentage of the estate, paid to the attorney and others who handle the probate proceeding.

Proving a Will - The process of establishing the validity of a will before the probate court. (See Self-Proving Will)

QTIP Trust - A Qualified Terminable Interest Trust (Q-Tip) is a type of trust which provides an unlimited marital deduction for qualified property put into the trust. However, rather than permitting the surviving spouse to have full power to distribute the property to anyone he or she wishes, the trust restricts the ability of the surviving spouse to distribute the property in the trust to a select group of individuals, such as the children, as agreed when both spouses were alive. Without the new QTIP laws, any attempt to "tie down" the property and restrict the surviving spouse's rights to transfer the trust property would have resulted in the property not qualifying for the marital deduction tax benefit.

Quitclaim Deed - A document (a deed) that transfers a person's interest in a piece of real estate, without the warranties or guarantees that are made in a warranty deed.

Revocable Living Trust - See Living Trust

Revocable Trust - A trust which can be amended or revoked by the person(s) who established the trust.

Real Property - Land and attachments to the land, such as buildings, fences, etc.

Right to Die - The right to decide not to have life prolonged by extraordinary, artificial means.

Rule Against Perpetuities - A rule of law limiting the duration of a trust. Some trusts can go on in perpetuity (forever), but most types of trusts have a maximum duration or life established by law.

Section 2053 Trust - A type of irrevocable trust, authorized by section 2503 of the IRS code, often established for children. Section 2503 allows annual gifts up to $10,000 to be made to the trust, rather than directly to the child, and still have the gift qualify for the $10,000 annual gift tax exclusion.

Self-Proving Will - A will which has been properly witnessed (by either two or three witnesses, depending on state laws) and the witnesses have signed an affidavit before a notary public stating that all of the proper formalities of the will's execution have been complied with. This usually makes it very easy for the court to "prove" the will.

Separate Property - In community property states, all property which is not held commonly by a married couple is considered separate property. In general, it is property owned by one spouse in which the other spouse does not own an interest.

Settlor - A person who establishes a trust. The term settlor is used interchangeably with the terms "trustor" and "grantor."

Simple Trust - Trusts that are established with terms that require the trust to "pay" all of its income out, so that it does not accumulate income on which income taxes would have to be paid.

Spendthrift - An individual who cannot handle money wisely and spends it wastefully.

Split Gift - Each spouse is entitled to give any individual $10,000 in a calendar year and, provided it is given properly, there is no tax consequence to the giver or receiver according to the "annual exclusion" laws. However, if a married couple tries to give more than $10,000 to an individual, they must file a gift-tax form declaring that the gift is split between them. If the form is not filed, the IRS cannot determine who gave the gift or gifts, and one member of the couple may be allocated the entire gift amount. Thus, he or she would actually owe a gift tax because his or her gift was over $10,000.

Springing Power - A power to act on the occurrence of some certain criteria, such as an illness or incompetency. The power is said to spring into existence upon the occurrence of the event. The agent's power to act for the principal under a durable power of attorney is usually a springing power.

Sprinkle or Sprinkling Power - The power given a trustee to decide how, when and why to distribute trust income to the trust's different beneficiaries. The sprinkling power allows the trustee to "sprinkle" the trust's income over the beneficiaries. It is a valuable power to give the trustee in irrevocable trusts because it allows the trustee to distribute income to the beneficiaries who will pay the smallest amount of income tax on the distribution.

Sprinkling Trust - A trust that grants the trustee a sprinkling power, which allows the trustee to decide how, when and why to distribute the trust income among the trust's beneficiaries.

Spouse - Legal term for husband or wife.

Stepped-up Basis - The new basis established for a property after the property has been evaluated and taxed as part of an estate. The new basis or "stepped-up basis" is the value of the property used to assess the estate tax.

Successor Trustee - The trustee who takes over when the initial trustee can no longer function.

Surviving Spouse - The husband or wife who lives after the death of his or her spouse.

Taxable Estate - The portion of an estate that is subject to federal estate taxes or state death taxes. Technically, all of an estate is subject to federal estate taxes; but, because of the unified credit, only estates with a value over the exemption equivalent amount actually have to pay any estate taxes. Therefore, it is common to refer to an estate with a value over the exemption equivalent amount as a taxable estate and an estate with a value under the exemption equivalent amount as a nontaxable estate.

Tenants by the Entirety - A way of owning property which, for almost all practical purposes, is the same as joint tenants. Tenancies by the entirety are creations of state law and are used only between husbands and wives, whereas joint tenancies can be used by anyone—not just by husbands and wives—who want to own property jointly.

Tenants in Common - A way of owning property in which two or more owners all "share" ownership of the property. The owners can own various percentages of the whole property, unlike joint tenants which each own an equal share. When one owner dies, his or her share does not "automatically" go to the other owner(s) because tenancies in common do not have a survivorship provision like joint tenancies.

Testamentary Trust - A trust created by a will.

Testate - One who dies leaving a will.

Title - Document proving ownership of property.

Totten Trust - A bank account that is designed to get around probate. The account is created by a person in his or her own name as the trustee for another person. It is a type of revocable trust until the creator dies, then it is paid out to the designated beneficiary(ies).

Trust - A legal document in which property is held and managed by a trustee for the benefit of another known as a beneficiary. A trust is a relationship in which property is held by one person for the benefit of another. The trust can be created verbally, but it will most often be in writing.

Trust Certificate - A summary, prepared by an attorney, of the trust's terms that evidences the trust exists.

Trust Corpus or Res - The property of a trust.

Trustee - The person or institution that manages the trust property under the terms of the trust.

Trustor - A person who establishes a trust. The term “trustor” is used interchangeably with the terms "settlor" and "grantor."

Unified Credit - A tax credit is given to each person by the IRS to be used during his or her life or after his or her death. The tax credit equals the amount of tax (gift or estate) which is assessed on the exemption equivalent value of property. It is considered the "unified" credit because it applies to both gift taxes and estate taxes and results from the IRS's effort to unify these two taxes or make them consistent.

It is often thought that the total value of taxed gifts and estate transfers can equal the exemption equivalent before any tax is assessed. This thought is wrong because a tax is actually assessed on the first dollar of taxable gift or estate property.

Note: Some property gifted is not exposed to the unified tax; for example, gifts that qualify for the annual gift tax exclusion are not considered exposed to the tax. Some property transferred in an estate is not exposed to the unified tax, such as property which goes to a spouse and qualifies for the unlimited marital deduction. Although a tax is assessed on gifts valued over the annual exclusion amount and on all the estate assets, the individual doesn't actually pay the tax on amounts up to the exemption equivalent maximum because the unified credit is applied against the tax.

Uniform Gift to Minors Act - A series of state statutes that provides a method for transferring property by gift to minors who cannot legally manage the property for themselves. The laws allow an adult to manage the property and yet not have it owned by the adult.

Uniform Probate Code - A standardized code designed by the American Law Institute to streamline the probate process. Many states have not adopted the code as part of their laws.

Unlimited Marital Deduction - The tax law that allows a person to give an unlimited value of property as a gift or leave an estate of unlimited value to his or her spouse without a gift or estate tax being assessed.

Warranty Deed - A deed which warrants that certain contracts will "run" (continue) with your property.

Will - A legal document stating the intentions of a deceased person concerning the distribution of his or her property and management of his or her affairs following his or her death. State law dictates the legality of a will.

INDEX

A

B

C

D

E

F

CPSIA information can be obtained at www.ICGtesting.com
Printed in the USA
BVOW05s1709300414

352176BV00018B/992/P

9 781935 723332